THE ULTRA SIMPLE
Bride's
WEDDING PLANNING GUIDE

From America's Top Wedding Experts,
Elizabeth & Alex Lluch

Authors of Over 3 Million Books Sold!

WS Publishing Group
San Diego, California

THE ULTRA SIMPLE BRIDE AND GROOM WEDDING PLANNING GUIDE

Elizabeth & Alex Lluch
America's Top Wedding Experts and
Authors of Over 3 Million Books Sold

Published by WS Publishing Group
San Diego, California 92119
Copyright © 2011 by WS Publishing Group

Cover photos: Karen French
www.karenfrenchphotography.com

For inquiries:
Log on to: www.WSPublishingGroup.com
E-mail: info@WSPublishingGroup.com

Printed in China

ISBN: 978-1-936061-23-5

CONTENTS

CONTENTS

INTRODUCTION

Congratulations on your engagement! You must be very excited to have found that special person with whom you will share your life! Planning a wedding is fun and exciting, but it can also be stressful. Grooms want to help with the numerous planning tasks, but they're not always sure how. WS Publishing Group created *The Ultra Simple Bride and Groom Wedding Planning Guide* to help couples plan their weddings together, from start to finish.

With *The Ultra Simple Bride and Groom Wedding Planning Guide*, you and your groom will have a complete guide to everything you need to do for your Big Day. This special two-book package, with one book just for the bride and one specifically for the groom, covers every important topic — from rings to attire to invitations to wedding party responsibilities to choosing the top vendors. Getting your fiancé involved and excited about wedding planning will be a breeze!

The Ultra Simple Bride and Groom Wedding Planning Guide includes a wedding planning checklist; detailed budget analysis; and Options, Things to Consider, Tips to Save Money, and Price Ranges for every aspect of the wedding. In addition, a section on wedding party responsibilities, a list of "Do's and Don'ts," traditional wedding formations, and more will be very helpful.

Finally, the groom's book contains a honeymoon section to help you choose your ideal destination and develop a comprehensive budget as you plan for the vacation of your dreams.

Your bride's book contains all the information you need to stay organized, while the groom's book completely outlines the areas in which your fiancé can help with planning and preparing for the wedding. You should each read your own books and share the information you learn while referring back to your wedding planning checklist.

We are confident that you will enjoy planning your wedding with the help of *The Ultra Simple Bride and Groom Wedding Planning Guide*. If you have anything else that you would like to see included in a future edition of this book, please write to us at: WS Publishing Group; 7290 Navajo Road, Suite 207; San Diego, California 92119. We listen to brides and grooms like you — that is why WS Publishing Group has become the best-selling publisher of wedding planners!

Sincerely,

Elizabeth H. Lluch

WEDDING PLANNING CHECKLIST

The following Wedding Planning Checklist itemizes everything you need to do or consider when planning your wedding and the best timeframe in which to accomplish each activity.

This checklist assumes that you have at least nine months to plan your wedding. If your wedding is in less than nine months, just start at the beginning of the list and try to catch up as quickly as you can!

Use the boxes to the left of the items to check off the activities as you accomplish them. This will enable you to see your progress and help you determine what has been done and what still needs to be done.

NINE MONTHS AND EARLIER

❑ Announce your engagement.

❑ Select a date for your wedding.

❑ Hire a professional wedding consultant.

❑ Determine the type of wedding you want:
location, formality, time of day, number of guests.

❑ Determine budget and how expenses will be shared.

❑ Develop a record-keeping system for payments made.

❑ Consolidate all guest lists: bride's, groom's,
bride's family, groom's family, and organize:
1) those who must be invited
2) those who should be invited
3) those who would be nice to invite

❑ Decide if you want to include children
among guests.

❑ Select and reserve ceremony site.

❑ Select and reserve your officiant.

❑ Select and reserve reception site.

❑ Select and order your bridal gown and headpiece.

❑ Determine color scheme.

❑ Select and book photographer.

❑ If ceremony or reception is at home, arrange for
home or garden improvements as needed.

NINE MONTHS AND EARLIER (CONT.)

❑ Use a calendar to note all important activities: showers, luncheons, parties, get-togethers, etc.

❑ Order passport, visa, or birth certificate, if needed, for your honeymoon or marriage license.

❑ Select maid of honor, best man, bridesmaids, and ushers (approximately one usher per 50 guests).

SIX TO NINE MONTHS BEFORE WEDDING

❑ Select flower girl and ring bearer.

❑ Give *Wedding Party Responsibility Cards* to your wedding party.

❑ Reserve wedding night bridal suite.

❑ Select attendants' dresses, shoes, and accessories.

❑ Select and book caterer, if needed.

❑ Select and book ceremony musicians.

❑ Select and book reception musicians or DJ.

❑ Schedule fittings and delivery dates for yourself, attendants, and flower girl.

❑ Select and book videographer.

❑ Select and book florist.

❑ Have engagement photos taken.

FOUR TO SIX MONTHS BEFORE WEDDING

❑ Start shopping for each other's wedding gifts.

❑ Reserve rental items needed for ceremony.

❑ Finalize guest list.

❑ Select and order wedding invitations, announcements, and other stationery such as thank-you notes, wedding programs, and seating cards.

❑ Address invitations or hire a calligrapher.

❑ Set date, time, and location for your rehearsal dinner.

❑ Arrange accommodations for out-of-town guests.

❑ Start planning your honeymoon.

❑ Select and book all miscellaneous services, i.e., gift attendant, valet parking, etc.

❑ Register for gifts.

❑ Purchase shoes and accessories.

❑ Begin to break in your shoes.

TWO TO FOUR MONTHS BEFORE WEDDING

❑ Select bakery and order wedding cake.

❑ Order party favors.

❑ Select and order room decorations.

❑ Purchase honeymoon attire and luggage.

TWO TO FOUR MONTHS BEFORE WEDDING (CONT.)

❑ Select and book transportation for wedding day.

❑ Check blood test and marriage license requirements.

❑ Shop for wedding rings and have them engraved.

❑ Consider having your teeth cleaned or bleached.

❑ Consider writing a will and/or prenuptial agreement.

❑ Plan activities for out-of-town guests both before and after the wedding.

❑ Purchase gifts for wedding attendants.

SIX TO EIGHT WEEKS BEFORE WEDDING

❑ Mail invitations. Include accommodation choices and a map to assist guests in finding the ceremony and reception sites.

❑ Maintain a record of RSVPs and all gifts received. Send thank-you notes upon receipt of gifts.

❑ Determine hairstyle and makeup.

❑ Schedule to have your hair, makeup, and nails done the day of the wedding.

❑ Finalize shopping for wedding day accessories such as toasting glasses, ring pillow, guest book, etc.

❑ Set up an area or a table in your home to display gifts as you receive them.

SIX TO EIGHT WEEKS BEFORE WEDDING (CONT.)

❑ Check with your local newspapers for wedding announcement requirements.

❑ Have your formal bridal portrait taken.

❑ Check requirements to change your name and address on your driver's license, social security card, insurance policies, subscriptions, bank accounts, etc.

❑ Select and reserve wedding attire for groom, ushers, ring bearer, and father of the bride.

❑ Select a guest book attendant. Decide where and when to have guests sign in.

❑ Mail invitations to rehearsal dinner.

❑ Get blood test and health certificate.

❑ Obtain marriage license.

❑ Plan a luncheon or dinner with your bridesmaids. Give them their gifts at that time or at the rehearsal dinner.

❑ Find "something old, something new, something borrowed, something blue, and a sixpence (or shiny penny) for your shoe."

❑ Finalize your menu, beverage, and alcohol order.

TWO TO SIX WEEKS BEFORE WEDDING

❑ Confirm ceremony details with your officiant.

❑ Arrange final fitting of bridesmaids' dresses.

❑ Have final fitting of your gown and headpiece.

❑ Make final floral selections.

❑ Finalize rehearsal dinner plans; arrange seating and write names on place cards, if desired.

❑ Make a detailed timeline for your wedding party.

❑ Make a detailed timeline for your service providers.

❑ Confirm details with all service providers, including attire. Give them copies of your wedding timeline.

❑ Start packing for your honeymoon.

❑ Finalize addressing and stamping announcements.

❑ Decide if you want to form a receiving line. If so, determine when and where to form the line.

❑ Contact guests who haven't responded.

❑ Pick up rings and check for fit.

❑ Meet with photographer and confirm special photos you want taken.

❑ Meet with videographer and confirm special events or people you want recorded.

TWO TO SIX WEEKS BEFORE WEDDING (CONT.)

❑ Meet with musicians and confirm music to be played during special events such as the first dance.

❑ Continue writing thank-you notes as gifts arrive.

❑ Remind bridesmaids and ushers of when and where to pick up their wedding attire.

❑ Purchase the lipstick, nail polish, and any other accessories you want your bridesmaids to wear.

❑ Determine ceremony seating for special guests. Give a list to the ushers.

❑ Plan reception room layout and seating with your reception site manager or caterer. Write names on place cards for arranged seating.

THE LAST WEEK

❑ Pick up wedding attire and make sure everything fits.

❑ Do final guest count and notify your caterer or reception site manager.

❑ Arrange for someone to drive the getaway car.

❑ Gather everything you will need for the rehearsal and wedding day.

❑ Review the schedule of events and last minute arrangements with your service providers. Give them each a detailed timeline.

THE LAST WEEK (CONT.)

❑ Familiarize yourself with guests' names. It will help during the receiving line and reception.

❑ Confirm all honeymoon reservations and accommodations. Pick up tickets and traveler's checks.

❑ Finish packing your suitcases for the honeymoon.

❑ Notify the post office to hold mail while you are away on your honeymoon.

THE REHEARSAL DAY

❑ Put suitcases in getaway car if leaving for your honeymoon the following day.

❑ Give your bridesmaids the lipstick, nail polish, and accessories you want them to wear for the wedding.

❑ Give best man the officiant's fee and any other checks for service providers. Instruct him to deliver these checks the day of the wedding.

❑ Arrange for someone to bring accessories such as flower basket, ring pillow, guest book and pen, toasting glasses, cake cutting knife, and napkins to the ceremony and reception.

❑ Arrange for someone to mail announcements the day after the wedding.

THE REHEARSAL DAY (CONT.)

❑ Arrange for someone to return rental items such as tuxedos, slip, and cake pillars after the wedding.

❑ Provide each member of your wedding party with a detailed schedule of events/timelines.

❑ Review ceremony seating with ushers.

THE WEDDING DAY

❑ Give the groom's ring to the maid of honor.

❑ Simply follow your detailed schedule of events.

❑ Relax and enjoy your wedding!

BUDGET ANALYSIS

This comprehensive Budget Analysis has been designed to provide you with all the expenses that can be incurred in any size wedding, including such hidden costs as taxes, gratuities, stamps, and other items that can easily add up to thousands of dollars in a wedding. After you have completed this budget, you will have a much better idea of what your wedding will cost. You can then prioritize and allocate your money accordingly.

This budget is divided into fifteen categories:
Ceremony, Wedding Attire, Photography, Videography, Stationery, Reception, Music, Bakery, Flowers, Decorations, Transportation, Rental Items, Gifts, Parties, and Miscellaneous.

At the beginning of each category is the percentage of a total wedding budget that is typically spent in that category, based on national averages. Multiply your intended wedding budget by this percentage and write that amount in the "Typically" space provided.

BUDGET ANALYSIS

To determine the total cost of your wedding, estimate the amount of money you will spend on each item in the budget analysis and write that amount in the "Budget" column after each item. Next to each expense item is the page number where you can find detailed information about it. Items printed in italics are traditionally paid for by the groom or his family.

Add all the "Budget" amounts within each category and write the total amount in the "Subtotal" space at the end of each category. Then add all the "Subtotal" figures to come up with your final wedding budget. The "Actual" column is for you to input your actual expenses as you purchase items or hire your service providers. Writing down the actual expenses will help you stay within your budget.

For example, if your total wedding budget is $20,000, write this amount at the top. To figure your typical ceremony expenses, multiply $20,000 by .05 (5%) to get $1,000. Write this amount on the "Typically" line in the "Ceremony" category to serve as a guide for all your ceremony expenses.

If you find, after adding up all your "Subtotals," that the total amount is more than what you had in mind to spend, simply decide which items are more important to you and adjust your expenses accordingly.

Items in italics are traditionally paid for by the groom or his family.

CEREMONY

- ❏ Ceremony Site Fee
- ❏ *Officiant's Fee*
- ❏ *Officiant's Gratuity*
- ❏ Guest Book/Pen/ Penholder
- ❏ Ring Bearer Pillow
- ❏ Flower Girl Basket

WEDDING ATTIRE

- ❏ Bridal Gown
- ❏ Alterations
- ❏ Headpiece/Veil
- ❏ Gloves
- ❏ Jewelry
- ❏ Garter/Stockings
- ❏ Shoes
- ❏ Hairdresser
- ❏ Makeup Artist
- ❏ Manicure/Pedicure
- ❏ *Groom's Formal Wear*

PHOTOGRAPHY

- ❏ Bride & Groom's Album
- ❏ Engagement Photograph
- ❏ Formal Bridal Portrait
- ❏ Parents' Album
- ❏ Proofs/Previews
- ❏ Digital Files
- ❏ Extra Prints

VIDEOGRAPHY

- ❏ Main Video
- ❏ Titles
- ❏ Extra Hours
- ❏ Photo Montage
- ❏ Extra Copies

STATIONERY

- ❏ Invitations
- ❏ Response Cards
- ❏ Reception Cards
- ❏ Ceremony Cards
- ❏ Pew Cards
- ❏ Seating/Place Cards
- ❏ Rain Cards
- ❏ Maps
- ❏ Ceremony Programs
- ❏ Announcements
- ❏ Thank-You Notes
- ❏ Stamps
- ❏ Calligraphy
- ❏ Napkins/Matchbooks

RECEPTION

- ❏ Reception Site Fee
- ❏ Hors d'Oeuvres
- ❏ Main Meal/Caterer
- ❏ Liquor/Beverages
- ❏ Bartending/Bar Setup Fee
- ❏ Corkage Fee
- ❏ Fee to Pour Coffee
- ❏ Gratuity

RECEPTION (CONT.)

- ❏ Service Providers' Meals
- ❏ Party Favors
- ❏ Disposable Cameras
- ❏ Rose Petals/Rice
- ❏ Gift Attendant
- ❏ Parking Fee/Valet Services

MUSIC

- ❏ Ceremony Music
- ❏ Reception Music

BAKERY

- ❏ Wedding Cake
- ❏ *Groom's Cake*
- ❏ Cake Delivery/Setup Fee
- ❏ Cake-Cutting Fee
- ❏ Cake Top
- ❏ Cake Knife/ Toasting Glasses

FLOWERS

BOUQUETS
- ❑ *Bride*
- ❑ Tossing
- ❑ Maid of Honor
- ❑ Bridesmaid

FLORAL HAIRPIECES
- ❑ Maid of Honor/
  Bridesmaids
- ❑ Flower Girl

CORSAGES
- ❑ *Bride's Going Away*
- ❑ *Family Members*

BOUTONNIERES
- ❑ *Groom*
- ❑ *Ushers/Other
  Family Members*

CEREMONY SITE
- ❑ Main Altar
- ❑ Altar Candelabra
- ❑ Aisle Pews

FLOWERS (CONT.)

RECEPTION SITE
- ❑ Head Table
- ❑ Guest Tables
- ❑ Buffet Table
- ❑ Punch Table
- ❑ Cake Table
- ❑ Cake
- ❑ Cake Knife
- ❑ Toasting Glasses
- ❑ Floral Delivery/Setup
  Fee

DECORATIONS

- ❑ Table Centerpieces
- ❑ Balloons

TRANSPORTATION

- ❑ Transportation

RENTAL ITEMS

- ❑ Bridal Slip
- ❑ Ceremony Accessories
- ❑ Tent/Canopy
- ❑ Dance Floor
- ❑ Tables/Chairs
- ❑ Linen/Tableware
- ❑ Heaters
- ❑ Lanterns
- ❑ Other Rental Items

GIFTS

- ❑ *Bride's Gift*
- ❑ Groom's Gift
- ❑ Bridesmaids' Gifts
- ❑ *Ushers' Gifts*

PARTIES

- ❑ Engagement Party
- ❑ *Bachelor Party*
- ❑ Bachelorette Party
- ❑ Bridal Shower
- ❑ Bridesmaids' Luncheon
- ❑ *Rehearsal Dinner*
- ❑ Day-After Brunch

MISCELLANEOUS

- ❑ Newspaper Announcements
- ❑ *Marriage License*
- ❑ *Prenuptial Agreement*
- ❑ Bridal Gown Preservation
- ❑ Bridal Bouquet Preservation
- ❑ Wedding Consultant
- ❑ Wedding Planning Online
- ❑ Taxes

Items in italics are traditionally paid for by the groom or his family.

WEDDING BUDGET	Budget	Actual
YOUR TOTAL WEDDING BUDGET	$	$
CEREMONY (Typically = 5% of Budget)	$	$
Ceremony Site Fee	$	$
Officiant's Fee	$	$
Officiant's Gratuity	$	$
Guest Book/Pen/Penholder	$	$
Ring Bearer Pillow	$	$
Flower Girl Basket	$	$
SUBTOTAL 1	$	$

WEDDING ATTIRE (Typically = 10% of Budget)	$	$
Bridal Gown	$	$
Alterations	$	$
Headpiece/Veil	$	$
Gloves	$	$
Jewelry	$	$
Garter/Stockings	$	$
Shoes	$	$
Hairdresser	$	$

WEDDING BUDGET	Budget	Actual
WEDDING ATTIRE (CONT.)		
Makeup Artist	$	$
Manicure/Pedicure	$	$
Groom's Formal Wear	$	$
SUBTOTAL 2	$	$

	Budget	Actual
PHOTOGRAPHY (Typically = 9% of Budget)	$	$
Bride & Groom's Album	$	$
Engagement Photograph	$	$
Formal Bridal Portrait	$	$
Parents' Album	$	$
Proofs/Previews	$	$
Digital Files	$	$
Extra Prints	$	$
SUBTOTAL 3	$	$

WEDDING BUDGET	Budget	Actual
VIDEOGRAPHY (Typically = 5% of Budget)	$	$
Main Video	$	$
Titles	$	$
Extra Hours	$	$
Photo Montage	$	$
Extra Copies	$	$
SUBTOTAL 4	$	$

STATIONERY (Typically = 4% of Budget)	$	$
Invitations	$	$
Response Cards	$	$
Reception Cards	$	$
Ceremony Cards	$	$
Pew Cards	$	$
Seating/Place Cards	$	$
Rain Cards	$	$
Maps	$	$
Ceremony Programs	$	$
Announcements	$	$

WEDDING BUDGET	Budget	Actual
STATIONERY (CONT.)		
Thank-You Notes	$	$
Stamps	$	$
Calligraphy	$	$
Napkins/Matchbooks	$	$
SUBTOTAL 5	$	$

	Budget	Actual
RECEPTION (Typically = 35% of Budget)	$	$
Reception Site Fee	$	$
Hors d'Oeuvres	$	$
Main Meal/Caterer	$	$
Liquor/Beverages	$	$
Bartending/Bar Setup Fee	$	$
Corkage Fee	$	$
Fee to Pour Coffee	$	$
Service Providers' Meals	$	$
Gratuity	$	$
Party Favors	$	$
Disposable Cameras	$	$

WEDDING BUDGET	Budget	Actual
RECEPTION (CONT.)		
Rose Petals/Rice	$	$
Gift Attendant	$	$
Parking Fee/Valet Services	$	$
SUBTOTAL 6	$	$

	Budget	Actual
MUSIC (Typically = 5% of Budget)	$	$
Ceremony Music	$	$
Reception Music	$	$
SUBTOTAL 7	$	$

	Budget	Actual
BAKERY (Typically = 2% of Budget)	$	$
Wedding Cake	$	$
Groom's Cake	$	$
Cake Delivery/Setup Fee	$	$
Cake-Cutting Fee	$	$
Cake Top	$	$
Cake Knife/Toasting Glasses	$	$
SUBTOTAL 8	$	$

WEDDING BUDGET	Budget	Actual
FLOWERS (Typically = 6% of Budget)	$	$
BOUQUETS	$	$
Bride	$	$
Tossing	$	$
Maid of Honor	$	$
Bridesmaids	$	$
FLORAL HAIRPIECES	$	$
Maid of Honor/Bridesmaids	$	$
Flower Girl	$	$
CORSAGES	$	$
Bride's Going Away	$	$
Family Members	$	$
BOUTONNIERES	$	$
Groom	$	$
Ushers/Other Family Members	$	$
CEREMONY SITE	$	$
Main Altar	$	$
Altar Candelabra	$	$
Aisle Pews	$	$

WEDDING BUDGET	Budget	Actual
FLOWERS (CONT.)		
RECEPTION SITE	$	$
Reception Site	$	$
Head Table	$	$
Guest Tables	$	$
Buffet Table	$	$
Punch Table	$	$
Cake Table	$	$
Cake	$	$
Cake Knife	$	$
Toasting Glasses	$	$
Floral Delivery/Setup Fee	$	$
SUBTOTAL 9	$	$

DECORATIONS (Typically = 3% of Budget)	$	$
Table Centerpieces	$	$
Balloons	$	$
SUBTOTAL 10	$	$

Budget Analysis ❖ 29

WEDDING BUDGET	Budget	Actual
TRANSPORTATION (Typically = 2% of Budget)	$	$
Transportation	$	$
SUBTOTAL 11	$	$

RENTAL ITEMS	Budget	Actual
RENTAL ITEMS (Typically = 3% of Budget)	$	$
Bridal Slip	$	$
Ceremony Accessories	$	$
Tent/Canopy	$	$
Dance Floor	$	$
Tables/Chairs	$	$
Linen/Tableware	$	$
Heaters	$	$
Lanterns	$	$
Other Rental Items	$	$
SUBTOTAL 12	$	$

WEDDING BUDGET	Budget	Actual
GIFTS (Typically = 3% of Budget)	$	$
Bride's Gift	$	$
Groom's Gift	$	$
Bridesmaids' Gifts	$	$
Ushers' Gifts	$	$
SUBTOTAL 13	$	$

PARTIES (Typically = 4% of Budget)	$	$
Engagement Party	$	$
Bridal Shower	$	$
Bachelor Party	$	$
Bachelorette Party	$	$
Bridesmaids' Luncheon	$	$
Rehearsal Dinner	$	$
Day-After Brunch	$	$
SUBTOTAL 14	$	$

WEDDING BUDGET	Budget	Actual
MISCELLANEOUS (Typically = 4% of Budget)	$	$
Newspaper Announcements	$	$
Marriage License	$	$
Prenuptial Agreement	$	$
Bridal Gown Preservation	$	$
Bridal Bouquet Preservation	$	$
Wedding Consultant	$	$
Wedding Planning Online	$	$
Taxes	$	$
SUBTOTAL 15	$	$

	Budget	Actual
GRAND TOTAL (Add "Budget" & "Actual" Subtotals 1-15)	$	$

ATTIRE & BEAUTY

Bridal gowns come in a wide variety of styles, materials, colors, lengths, and prices. You should order your gown at least four to six months before your wedding if your gown has to be ordered and then fitted. In selecting your gown, keep in mind the time of year and formality of your wedding. It is a good idea to look at bridal magazines to compare the various styles and colors. If you see a gown you like, call boutiques in your area to see if they carry that line. Always try on a gown before ordering it.

BRIDAL GOWN

Options: Different gown styles complement different body types. Here are some tips when choosing your dress:

- **A short, heavy figure:** To look taller and slimmer, avoid knit fabrics. Use the princess or A-line style. Chiffon produces a floating effect and can camouflage weight, although a short bride can get lost in a ballgown. A sturdy fabric like silk shantung or taffeta can hide weight as well.

- **A short, thin figure:** An empire waist or natural waist style with bouffant skirt or classic sheath will produce a taller, more rounded figure. Chiffon and lace are good fabric choices.

- **A tall, heavy figure:** Princess or A-line styles are best for slimming the figure. Avoid clingy fabrics and note that an empire waist may draw attention to a big bust. Chiffon and lace fabrics are recommended.

- **A tall, thin figure:** Tiers, runching or flounces will complement a tall bride. A simple silhouette will look elegant; just be sure sleeves and hems are the right length. Satin, silk and lace are the best fabrics.

The guidelines below will help you select the most appropriate gown for your wedding:

Informal wedding:
Street-length or tea-length gown
No veil or train
Corsage or small bouquet

Semiformal wedding:
Floor-length gown
Chapel train
Fingertip veil
Small bouquet

Formal daytime wedding:
Floor-length gown
Chapel or sweep train
Fingertip veil or hat
Gloves
Medium-sized bouquet

Formal evening wedding:
Same as formal daytime
except longer veil

Very formal wedding:
Floor-length gown
Cathedral train
Full-length veil
Elaborate headpiece
Long sleeves or long gloves
Cascading bouquet

Things to Consider: When ordering a gown, make sure you order the correct size. If you are between sizes, order the larger one. You can always have your gown tailored down to fit, but it is not always possible to have it enlarged or to lose enough weight to fit into it! Don't forget to ask when your gown will arrive, and be sure to get this in writing. The gown should arrive at least six weeks before the wedding so you can have it tailored and select the appropriate accessories to complement it.

It's a good idea to put on "evening" makeup before going to try on dresses — trying on your wedding gown with a plain face is like trying on an evening dress wearing sneakers!

Some gown manufacturers suggest ordering a size larger than needed. This requires more alterations, which may mean extra charges. It is a good idea to locate a few tailors in your area and ask for alteration pricing in advance.

Many boutiques offer tailoring services, but you will often find a better price by finding an independent tailor specializing in bridal gown alterations. Also, gowns often fail to arrive on time, creating unnecessary stress for you. Be sure to order your gown with enough time to allow for delivery delays and also be sure to check the reputation of the boutique before buying.

Tips to Save Money: Consider renting a gown or buying one secondhand. Renting a gown usually costs about 40 to 60 percent of its retail price. Consider this practical option if you are not planning to preserve the gown. The disadvantage of renting, however, is that your options are more limited.

Ask about discontinued styles and gowns. Watch for clearances and sales, or buy your gown "off the rack." Restore or refurbish a family heirloom gown. If you have a friend, sister, or other family member who is planning a wedding, consider purchasing a gown that you could both wear. Change the veil and headpiece to personalize it.

Price Range: $500 - $10,000

ALTERATIONS

Things to Consider: Alterations usually require several

fittings. Allow four to six weeks for alterations to be completed. However, do not alter your gown months before the wedding. Your weight may fluctuate during the final weeks of planning, and the gown might not fit properly. Alterations are usually not included in the cost of the gown.

You may also want to consider making some modifications to your gown such as shortening or lengthening the train, customizing the sleeves, beading and so forth. Ask your bridal boutique what they charge for the modifications you are considering.

Tips to Save Money: Consider hiring an independent tailor. Their fees are usually lower than bridal boutiques.

Price Range: $75 - $500

HEADPIECE/VEIL

The headpiece is the part of the bride's outfit to which the veil is attached.

Options for Headpieces: Bow, Garden Hat, Headband, Mantilla, Pillbox, Pouf, Tiara

Options for Veils: Ballet, Bird Cage, Blusher, Cathedral

Length, Chapel Length, Fingertip, Flyaway

Things to Consider: The headpiece should complement but not overshadow your gown. In addition to the headpiece, you might want a veil. Veils come in different styles and lengths.

Select a length which complements the length of your train. Consider the total look you're trying to achieve with your gown, headpiece, veil, and hairstyle. If possible, schedule your hair "test appointment" the day you go veil shopping — you'll be able to see how your veil looks on your hairstyle.

Tips to Save Money: Some boutiques offer a free headpiece or veil with the purchase of a gown. Make sure you ask for this before purchasing your gown.

Or, you may be able to purchase an inexpensive headpiece or veil from an online retailer. Bridal boutique prices may be inflated.

Price Range: $20 - $500

GLOVES

Gloves add a nice touch to either short-sleeved, three-quarter length, or sleeveless gowns.

Options: Gloves come in various styles and lengths. Depending on the length of your sleeves, select gloves that reach above your elbow, just below your elbow, halfway between your wrist and elbow, or only to your wrist.

Things to Consider: You should not wear gloves if your gown has long sleeves, or if you're planning a small, at-home wedding.

Price Range: $15 - $100

JEWELRY

Jewelry can beautifully accent your dress and be the perfect finishing touch.

Options: Select pieces of jewelry that can be classified as "something old, something new, something borrowed, or something blue."

Things to Consider: Brides look best with just a few pieces of jewelry — perhaps a pendant necklace or string of pearls and earrings with a simple bracelet. If your dress has a lot of beading or embellishments, keep jewelry understated.

Purchase complementary jewelry for your bridesmaids, to match the colors of their dresses. This will give your bridal party a coordinated look.

Price Range: $60 - $2,000

GARTER

It is customary for the bride to wear a garter just above the knee on her wedding day. After the bouquet tossing ceremony, the groom takes the garter off the bride's leg. All the single men gather on the dance floor. The groom then tosses the garter to them over his back. According to age-old tradition, whoever catches the garter is the next to be married!

Things to Consider: You will need to choose the proper music for this event. A popular and fun song to play during the garter removal ceremony is *The Stripper*, by David Rose.

Price Range: $15 - $60

SHOES

Things to Consider: Make sure you select comfortable

shoes that complement your gown. Don't forget to break them in well before your wedding day. Tight shoes can make you miserable.

Price Range: $50 - $500

HAIR

Many brides prefer to have their hair professionally arranged with their headpiece the day of the wedding rather than trying to do it themselves.

Things to Consider: Have your professional hairdresser experiment with your hair and headpiece before your wedding day so there are no surprises. Most hairdressers will include the cost of a sample session in your package. They will try several styles on you and write down the specifics of each one so that things go quickly and smoothly on your wedding day. On the big day, you can go to the salon or have the stylist meet you at your home or dressing site. Consider having him or her arrange your bridal party's hair for a consistent look.

Tips to Save Money: Negotiate having your hair arranged free of charge or at a discount in exchange for bringing your mother, your fiancé's mother, and your bridal party to the salon.

Price Range: $50 - $200 per person

MAKEUP

A professional makeup artist will apply makeup that should last throughout the day and will often provide you with samples for touch-ups.

Things to Consider: It's smart to go for a trial run before the day of the wedding so there are no surprises. You can either go to the salon or have the makeup artist meet you at your home or dressing site. Consider having him or her apply makeup for your mother, your fiancé's mother, and your bridesmaids for a consistent look. In selecting a makeup artist, make sure he or she has been trained in makeup for photography. It is very important to wear the proper amount of makeup for photographs.

Consider having your makeup trial right before your hairdresser trial — that way you'll see how your hair looks with your makeup on. It can make a big difference.

Your makeup artist may want you to bring a few of your own products to avoid the spread of bacteria, including mascara and lipstick.

Tips to Save Money: Try to negotiate having your makeup

applied free of charge or at a discount in exchange for bringing your mother, your fiancé's mother, and your wedding party to the makeup artist.

Price Range: $20 - $150 per person

MANICURE/PEDICURE

As a final touch, it's nice to have a professional manicure and/or pedicure the day of your wedding.

Things to Consider: Don't forget to bring the appropriate color nail polish with you for your appointment. You can either go to the salon or have the manicurist meet you at your home or dressing site. Consider having him or her give your mother, your fiancé's mother, and your bridesmaids a manicure in the same color.

Make sure you have a bottle of the nail color you choose in case of chips.

Tips to Save Money: Try to negotiate getting a manicure or pedicure free of charge or at a discount in exchange for bringing your mother, your fiancé's mother, and your wedding party to the salon.

Price Range: $15 - $75 per person

NOTES

_____

_____

_____

_____

_____

_____

_____

_____

_____

_____

_____

_____

_____

_____

_____

_____

_____

_____

_____

_____

_____

_____

_____

_____

_____

_____

_____

_____

_____

CEREMONY

CEREMONY SITE FEE

The ceremony site fee is the fee to rent a facility for your wedding. In churches, cathedrals, chapels, temples, or synagogues, this fee may include the organist, wedding coordinator, custodian, changing rooms for the bridal party, and miscellaneous items such as kneeling cushions, aisle runner, and candelabra. Be sure to ask what the site fee includes prior to booking a facility. Throughout this book, the word church will be used to refer to the site where the ceremony will take place.

Options: Churches, cathedrals, chapels, temples, synagogues, private homes, gardens, hotels, clubs, halls, parks, museums, yachts, wineries, beaches

Things to Consider: Your selection of a ceremony site will be influenced by the formality of your wedding, the season of the year, the number of guests expected and your religious affiliation. Make sure you ask about restrictions or guidelines regarding photography, videography, music, decorations, candles, and rice or rose petal-tossing. Consider issues such as proximity of the ceremony site to the reception site, parking availability, handicapped accessibility, and time constraints.

Tips to Save Money: Have your ceremony at the same facility as your reception to save a second rental fee. Set a realistic guest list and stick to it. Hire an experienced wedding consultant. At a church or temple, ask if there is another wedding that day and share the cost of floral decorations with that bride. Membership in a church, temple, or club can reduce rental fees. At a garden wedding, have guests stand and omit the cost of renting chairs.

Price Range: $100 - $1,000

GUEST BOOK/PEN/PENHOLDER

The guest book is a formal register that your guests sign as they arrive at the ceremony or reception. It serves as a memento of who attended your wedding. This book is often placed outside the ceremony or reception site, along with an elegant pen and penholder. A guest book attendant is responsible for inviting all guests to sign in. A younger sibling or close friend who is not part of the wedding party may be well-suited for this position.

Options: There are many styles of guest books, pens, and penholders to choose from. Some books have space for your guests to write a short note to the bride and groom.

Things to Consider: Make sure you have more than one pen in case one runs out of ink. If you are planning a large ceremony (over 300 guests), consider having more than one book and pen so that your guests don't have to wait in line to sign in.

Price Range: $30 - $100

RING BEARER PILLOW

The ring bearer, usually a boy between the ages of 4 and 8, carries the bride and groom's rings or mock rings on a pillow. He follows the maid of honor and precedes the flower girl or bride in the processional.

Options: These pillows come in many styles and colors. You can find them at most gift shops and bridal boutiques.

Things to Consider: If the ring bearer is very young (less than 7 years), place mock rings on the pillow in place of the real rings to prevent losing them. If mock rings are used, instruct your ring bearer to put the pillow upside down during the recessional so your guests don't see them.

Tips to Save Money: Make your own ring bearer pillow by taking a small white pillow and attaching a pretty ribbon to it to hold the rings.

Price Range: $15 - $75

FLOWER GIRL BASKET

The flower girl, usually between the ages of 4 and 8, carries a basket filled with flowers, rose petals, or paper rose petals to scatter as she walks down the aisle. She follows the ring bearer or maid of honor and precedes the bride during the processional.

Options: You can find baskets at most florists, gift shops, and bridal boutiques.

Things to Consider: Discuss any restrictions regarding rose petal, flower, or paper-tossing with your ceremony site. Select a basket which complements your guest book and ring bearer pillow. If the flower girl is very young (less than 7 years), consider giving her a small bouquet instead of a flower basket.

Tips to Save Money: Ask your florist if you can borrow a basket and attach a pretty white bow to it.

Price Range: $20 - $75

UNIQUE CEREMONY IDEAS

IDEAS TO PERSONALIZE YOUR CEREMONY

Regardless of your religious affiliation, there are numerous ways in which you can personalize your wedding ceremony to add a more creative touch. If you're planning a religious ceremony at a church or temple, be sure to discuss all ideas with your officiant.

The following list incorporates some ideas to personalize your wedding ceremony:

- Invite your mother to be part of the processional. Have her walk down the aisle with the groom and his father. (This is the traditional Jewish processional.)
- Invite the groom's parents to be part of the processional as well.
- Ask friends and family members to perform special readings.
- Incorporate poetry and/or literature into your readings.

- Ask a friend or family member with musical talent to perform at the ceremony.
- Change places with the officiant and face your guests during the ceremony.
- Light a unity candle to symbolize your two lives joining together as one.
- Drink wine from a shared "loving" cup to symbolize bonding with each other.
- Hand a rose to each of your mothers as you pass by them during the recessional.
- Release white doves into the air after being pronounced "husband and wife."
- If the ceremony is held outside on a grassy area, have your guests toss grass or flower seeds over you instead of rice.
- Publicly express gratitude for all that your parents have done for you.
- Burn incense to give the ceremony an exotic feeling.
- Use a canopy to designate an altar for a non-church setting. Decorate it in ways that are symbolic or meaningful to you.

IDEAS TO PERSONALIZE YOUR MARRIAGE VOWS

Regardless of your religious affiliation and whether you're planning a church or outdoor ceremony, there are ways in which you can personalize your marriage vows to make them more meaningful for you. As with all your ceremony plans, be sure to discuss your ideas for marriage vows with your officiant.

The following are some ideas that you might want to consider when planning your marriage vows:

- You and your fiancé could write your own personal marriage vows and keep them secret from one another until the actual ceremony.
- Incorporate your guests and family members into your vows by acknowledging their presence at the ceremony.
- Describe what you cherish most about your partner and what you hope for your future together.
- Describe your commitment to and love for one another.
- Discuss your feelings and beliefs about marriage.
- If either of you has children from a previous marriage, mention these children in your vows and discuss your mutual love for and commitment to them.

NOTES

_____

_____

_____

_____

_____

_____

_____

_____

_____

_____

_____

_____

_____

_____

_____

_____

_____

_____

_____

_____

_____

_____

_____

_____

_____

_____

_____

_____

_____

_____

PHOTOGRAPHY

The photographs taken at your wedding are the best way to preserve your special day. Chances are you and your fiancé will look at the photos many times during your lifetime. Therefore, hiring a good photographer is one of the most important tasks in planning your wedding.

BRIDE & GROOM'S ALBUM

The bride and groom's photo album contain the most photographs and will be looked at repeatedly over the years. Choosing a photographer who will shoot your wedding in the style you want and deliver the shots you want is an important task. Photography packages come in a very wide range of prices and services.

Options: Photographers will tell you that they're skilled in "photo journalistic," "candid" or "editorial" style photography, so look through their portfolios for the style that stands out to you. Some photographers are known for formal poses, while others specialize in more candid, creative shots. Some can capture both.

The industry standard for wedding photographers is now digital film, which is the easiest to print, retouch, and allows the photographer to get the most shots to choose from. However, some photographers still like to use film, or a combination of digital and film. Film forces the photographer to choose and set up each shot carefully and artfully and produces a timeless, romantic and textured photograph. Decide which look and feel you want for your photos.

You also want to inquire as to whether your desired photographer works alone or with a backup shooter or assistant. Having more than one person shooting the wedding means you will have a wider variety of shots, especially candids and special moments that one person could miss. Many times a second photographer will be included in the price of the package.

Finally, there are a large variety of wedding albums. They vary in size, color, material, construction and price. Traditional-style albums frame each individual photo in a mat on the page. Digitally designed "Montage" albums group the photos in a creatively designed fashion for a more modern look. Find one that you like and will feel proud of showing to your friends and family. Some of the most popular manufacturers of wedding albums are Art Leather, Leather Craftsman, Capri and Renaissance.

Different papers are also available to print your photos — pearl and metallic as well as black and white can be chosen. Ask to see samples.

Compare at least three photographers for quality, value, and price. Be aware that novice photographers or those who shoot weddings "on the side" are less expensive, but the quality of their photographs may not be as good as a wedding professional. For many couples on budgets, the photography was the area in which they splurged in order to have the best wedding album possible.

Things to Consider: It is always best to hire a photographer who specializes in weddings. Your photographer should be experienced in wedding procedures and familiar with your ceremony and reception sites. This will allow him or her to anticipate your next move and be in the proper place at the right time to capture all the special moments. However, personal rapport is extremely important. The photographer may be an expert, but if you don't feel comfortable or at ease with him or her, your photography will reflect this. Comfort and compatibility with your photographer can make or break your wedding day and your photographs!

Look at his or her work. See if the photographer captured the excitement and emotion of the bridal couple. Also, remember that the wedding album should unfold like a story book of the wedding day.

PHOTOGRAPHY

Consider having a "First Look" session, which is when the bride and groom opt to see each other right before the ceremony. The photographer captures this special, intimate moment, making for beautiful photos. Many couples love First Looks because it puts them at ease before walking down the aisle, as well allows them to skip lengthy portrait sessions between the ceremony and reception. They get to have a private moment together and spend more time with their guests after the ceremony.

When comparing photographer prices, compare the quantity and size of the photographs in your album and the type of album that each photographer will use. Ask how many photos will be taken on average at a wedding of your size. Some photographers do not work with proofs. Rather, they simply supply you with a finished album after the wedding. Doing this may reduce the cost of your album but will also reduce your selection of photographs. Many photographers will put your proofs on a DVD for viewing. This is much less bulky and an easy way to preview all of your wedding photos.

Make sure the photographer you interview is the specific person who will photograph your wedding. Many companies have more than one photographer. The more professional companies will make sure that you meet with (and view the work of) the photographer who will photograph your wedding. This way you can get an idea of his or her style and personality and begin to establish a rapport with your photographer. Your chosen photographer's name should go on your contract!

Also, some churches do not allow photographs to be shot during the ceremony. Please find out the rules and present them to your photographer so he or she is knowledgeable about your site.

Tips to Save Money: Consider hiring a professional photographer for the formal shots of your ceremony only. You can then ask your guests take candid shots and create an online photo album where they can post their favorite shots.

Select a photographer who charges a flat fee to shoot the wedding and allows you to purchase the photos on a DVD.

Ask for specials and package deals. Your photographer may be willing to negotiate to get your business, but you won't know if you don't ask.

Price Range: $900 - $9,000

ENGAGEMENT PHOTOGRAPH

Many couples are interested in a set of engagement photos to accompany their wedding-day photography. These make a nice keepsake for you, as well as a gift for friends and family. If taken far enough in advance, you can even include these photos in your Save the Date cards.

Options: Most couples prefer to have engagement photos taken outside and not in a studio. Ask your photographer if he or she can scout locations, or you can choose a meaningful spot. Locations like the beach, a favorite outdoor café, your university, a park, a beautiful field, or even your own home make for nice photos. Discuss with your photographer whether you want candid shots or posed portrait shots or a combination of both.

Things to Consider: On the day of the shoot, bring more than one wardrobe change and wear nice shoes, as many shots will be full-body. Engagement shoots usually include affectionate shots such as the couple hugging or even kissing, so talk to your partner about what you're both comfortable with. Finally, ask your photographer to take some classic bridal portraits (shots of just bride). Modernly, many engagement shoots also include props, such as a picnic blanket, books, balloons, your dog — anything that you can have fun with or that represents you as a couple. Discuss with your groom what you want to incorporate.

Tips to Save Money: Consider hiring the same photographer for engagement photos as for the wedding; many will build the price into the total photography package.

To really cut costs, ask a friend or family member to take photos of you and your fiancé.

Price Range: $75 - $300

FORMAL BRIDAL PORTRAIT

You may want a studio bridal portrait taken a few weeks before the wedding. Traditionally, this photo was sent to the newspaper to announce a marriage; however, few newspapers still accept these announcements.

Things to Consider: Some fine bridal salons provide an attractive background where the bride may arrange to have her formal bridal photograph taken after the final fitting of her gown. This will save you the hassle of bringing your gown and headpiece to the photographer's studio and dressing up once again.

Tips to Save Money: Consider having your formal portrait taken the day of your wedding. This will save you the studio costs and the hassle of getting dressed for the photo.

Price Range: $75 - $300

PARENTS' ALBUM

The parents' album is a smaller version of the bride and groom's album. It usually contains about twenty 5x7" photographs. Photos should be carefully selected for each individual family. If given as a gift, the album can be personalized with the bride and groom's names and date of their wedding on the front cover. Small coffeetable-style books can also be created from digital files that are montaged onto the pages. Ask to see samples of different types of parent albums available.

Tips to Save Money: Try to negotiate at least one free parents' album with the purchase of the bride and groom's album.

Price Range: $100 - $600

PROOFS/PREVIEWS

Proofs/previews or proof DVDs are the preliminary prints or digital images from which the bride and groom select photographs for their album and for their parents' albums. The prints vary from 4x5" to 5x5" and 4x6". The DVD allows you to view your photos on a screen in a larger size and more detail.

Things to Consider: When selecting a package, ask how many photos the photographer will take. The more images, the wider the selection you will have to choose from. For a wide selection, the photographer must take at least 3 to 5 times the number of prints that will go into your album. Ask the photographer how soon after the wedding you will get your proofs. Request this in writing. Ideally, the proofs will be ready by the time you get back from your honeymoon.

Tips to Save Money: Ask your photographer to use your proofs as part of your album package to save developing costs.

Price Range: $100 - $600

DIGITAL FILES & EXTRA PRINTS

Most digital files are "jpegs," which is the file type that most labs use to make prints.

Extra prints are photographs ordered in addition to the main album or parents' albums. These are usually purchased as gifts for the bridal party, close friends and family members. Most photographers will not sell you the digital files up front since they hope to make a profit on selling extra prints after the wedding.

Things to Consider: It is important to discuss the cost of extra prints with your photographer since prices vary considerably. Knowing what extra prints will cost ahead of time will help you know if the photographer is truly within your budget. Ask the photographers you interview how long they keep the files and at what point they will become available to you. A professional photographer should keep a backup copy of the digital files for at least 10 years. Once you own your digital files, make a back-up copy of your disk every 5 or 6 years, as CDs and DVDs can deteriorate after 8 years or so.

Tips to Save Money: Many photographers will sell you the entire set of digital files after all photos have been ordered by family and friends. Often the price will vary, depending on the amount spent on re-orders. You can then make as many prints as you wish for a fraction of the cost.

Price Range: $100 - $800

PHOTOGRAPHY SHOT LIST

Discuss with your photographer the photos you want and create a shot list to ensure that your photographer captures the "must-haves." A good wedding photographer will plan the day with you to ensure that all the important moments are covered.

Check off your desired shots on the following list:

PRE-CEREMONY PHOTOGRAPHS

- ❑ Bride leaving her house
- ❑ Wedding rings with the invitation
- ❑ Bride getting dressed for the ceremony
- ❑ Bride looking at her bridal bouquet
- ❑ Maid of honor putting garter on bride's leg
- ❑ Bride by herself
- ❑ Bride with her mother
- ❑ Bride with her father
- ❑ Bride with mother and father
- ❑ Bride with her entire family and/or any combination thereof
- ❑ Bride with her maid of honor
- ❑ Bride with her bridesmaids
- ❑ Bride with the flower girl and/or ring bearer
- ❑ Bride's mother putting on her corsage
- ❑ Groom leaving his house
- ❑ Groom putting on his boutonniere
- ❑ Groom with his mother
- ❑ Groom with his father
- ❑ Groom with mother and father
- ❑ Groom with his entire family and/or any combination thereof
- ❑ Groom with his best man
- ❑ Groom with his ushers

PHOTOGRAPHY CHECKLIST

❏ Groom with the bride's father
❏ Bride and her father getting out of the limousine
❏ Special members of the family being seated
❏ Groom waiting for the bride before the processional
❏ Bride and her father just before the processional

OTHER PRE-CEREMONY PHOTOGRAPHS

❏ _____

❏ _____

❏ _____

❏ _____

CEREMONY PHOTOGRAPHS

❏ The processional
❏ Bride and groom saying their vows
❏ Bride and groom exchanging rings
❏ Groom kissing the bride at the altar
❏ The recessional

OTHER CEREMONY PHOTOGRAPHS

❏ _____

❏ _____

❏ _____

❏ _____

POST-CEREMONY PHOTOGRAPHS

- ❑ Bride and groom
- ❑ Newlyweds with both of their families
- ❑ Newlyweds with the entire wedding party
- ❑ Bride and groom signing the marriage certificate
- ❑ Flowers and other decorations

OTHER POST-CEREMONY PHOTOGRAPHS

- ❑ _____
- ❑ _____
- ❑ _____
- ❑ _____

RECEPTION PHOTOGRAPHS

- ❑ Entrance of newlyweds and wedding party into the reception site
- ❑ Receiving line
- ❑ Guests signing the guest book
- ❑ Toasts
- ❑ First dance
- ❑ Bride and her father dancing
- ❑ Groom and his mother dancing
- ❑ Bride dancing with groom's father
- ❑ Groom dancing with bride's mother
- ❑ Wedding party and guests dancing

PHOTOGRAPHY CHECKLIST

❑ Cake table
❑ Cake-cutting ceremony
❑ Couple feeding each other cake
❑ Buffet table and its decoration
❑ Bouquet-tossing ceremony
❑ Garter-tossing ceremony
❑ Musicians
❑ The wedding party table
❑ The family tables
❑ Candid shots of your guests
❑ Bride and groom saying goodbye to their parents
❑ Bride and groom looking back, waving goodbye in
the getaway car

OTHER RECEPTION PHOTOGRAPHS

❑ _____

❑ _____

❑ _____

❑ _____

VIDEOGRAPHY

Next to your photo album, videography is the best way to preserve your wedding memories. Unlike photographs, videography captures the mood of the wedding day in motion and sound. Getting a wedding on video used to mean bright lights, cables, microphones and huge obtrusive cameras. But technology has changed, and today's videographers have more advanced equipment that allows them to film ceremonies with minimal disruption.

Today's wedding videos can also be edited and professionally produced, with music, slow motion, black and white scenes and many other special features. You have the option of selecting one, two, or three cameras to record your wedding. The more cameras used, the more action your videographer can capture — and the more expensive the service. An experienced videographer, however, can do a good job with just one camera.

Options: There are two basic types of wedding video production: documentary and cinematic. The documentary type production records your wedding day as it happened, in real time. Very little editing or embellishment is involved. These types of videos are normally less expensive and can be delivered within days after the wedding.

The cinematic type production is more reminiscent of a movie. Although it can be shot with one camera, most good cinematic wedding videos are shot with two cameras, allowing one videographer to focus on the events as they happen while the other gathers footage that will be added later to enhance the final result. This type of video requires more time due to the extensive editing of the footage, which can take up to 40 hours of studio time.

You may wish to have both of these — one straightforward version and another version with all the details and a nice, theatrical flow.

The latest technology includes the option of producing video in high definition. More televisions are being manufactured with high definition resolution, which delivers a much sharper picture than traditional sets. In years to come, viewers will encounter problems watching regular DVDs on their hi-def television sets. Standard definition video appears fuzzy and pixilated on the new high definition monitors. Having your ceremony shot in high definition will ensure that you'll be able to enjoy watching your wedding video in a crisp, clear resolution for years to come.

MAIN VIDEO

You will need to choose the type of video you want. Do you want the footage edited down to a 30-minute film, or do you want an "as it happened" replay? Remember, an edited video will require more time and will therefore be more expensive than just a documentary of the events.

Things to Consider: Be sure to hire a videographer who specializes in weddings and ask to see samples of his or her work. Weddings are very specialized events. A $1,000 video camera in the hands of a seasoned professional "wedding" videographer will produce far better results than a $3,000 broadcast quality camera or a $4,000 high definition camera in the hands of just an average camera operator. When considering a particular videographer, look at previous weddings the videographer has done. Notice the color and brightness of the screen, as well as the quality of sound. This will indicate the quality of his or her equipment. Note whether the picture is smooth or jerky. This will indicate the videographer's skill level. Ask about special effects such as titles, dissolve, and multiple screens. Find out what's included in the cost of your package so that there are no surprises at the end!

VIDEOGRAPHY

If you will be getting married in a church, find out the church's policies regarding videography. Some churches might require the videographer to film the ceremony from a specific distance.

As in photography, there are many companies with more than one videographer. These companies may use the work of their best videographer to sell their packages and then send a less experienced videographer to the wedding. Be sure to interview the videographer who will shoot your wedding so you can get a good idea of his or her style and personality. Ask to see his or her own work.

Tips to Save Money: Compare videographers' quality, value, and price. There is a wide range, and the most expensive is not necessarily the best. The videographer who uses one camera (instead of multiple cameras) is usually the most cost effective and may be all you need.

Consider hiring a company that offers both videography and photography. You might save money by combining the two services.

Ask a family member or close friend to record your wedding. However, realize that without professional equipment and expertise, the final product may not be as polished.

Price Range: $600 - $4,000

TITLES

Titles and subtitles can be edited into your video before or after the filming. Titles are important since twenty years from now you might not remember the exact time of your wedding or the names of your bridal party members. Some videographers charge more for titling. Make sure you discuss this with your videographer and get in writing exactly what titles will be included.

Options: Titles can include the date, time, and location of the wedding, the bride and groom's names, and the names of special members of the family and bridal party. Titles may also include special thanks to those who helped with the wedding. You can then send these people copies of your video, which would be a very appropriate and inexpensive gift!

Tips to Save Money: Consider asking for limited titles, such as only the names of the bride and groom and the date and time of the wedding.

Price Range: $50 - $300

EXTRA HOURS

Find out how much your videographer would charge to stay longer than the contracted time. Do this in case your reception lasts longer than expected. Don't forget to get this fee in writing.

Tips to Save Money: To avoid paying for hours beyond what's included in your selected package, calculate the maximum number of hours you think you'll need and negotiate that number of hours into your package price.

To reduce the amount of time you'll need to use the videographer, consider recording the ceremony only.

Price Range: $35 - $150 per hour

PHOTO MONTAGE

A photo montage is a series of photographs set to music on video. The number of photographs in your photo montage depends on the length of the songs and the amount of time allotted for each photograph. A typical song usually allows for thirty to forty photographs. Photo montages are a great way to display and reproduce your photographs. Copies of this video can be made for considerably less than the cost of reproducing photos.

Options: Your photo montage can include photos of you and your fiancé growing up in addition to shots from your rehearsal, wedding day, honeymoon, or any combination.

Things to Consider: Send copies of your photo montage video to close friends and family members as mementos of your wedding.

Tips to Save Money: There are many websites that allow you to create your own photo montage either for free or at a very low price. You can then transfer your photo montage to a DVD.

Price Range: $60 - $300

EXTRA COPIES

A videographer can produce higher quality copies than you can. Ask your videographer what the charge is for extra copies.

Tips to Save Money: You can burn a copy of your wedding DVD on your computer. Before making your own copies of your wedding video, be sure to ask your videographer if that is acceptable. Many contracts prohibit it, and doing so could be copyright infringement. Further, your videographer may have put a security device on the DVD that would prevent you from being able to copy it.

Price Range: $15 - $50

NOTES

_____

_____

_____

_____

_____

_____

_____

_____

_____

_____

_____

_____

_____

_____

_____

_____

_____

_____

_____

_____

_____

_____

_____

_____

_____

_____

_____

_____

STATIONERY

Begin creating your guest list as soon as possible. Ask your parents and the groom's parents for a list of people they would like to invite. You and your fiancé should make your own lists. Make certain that all names are spelled correctly and that all addresses are current. Determine if you wish to include children; if so, add their names to your list. All children over the age of 16 should receive their own invitation.

A complete guide to creating your guest list is found in the groom's book.

INVITATIONS

Order your invitations at least four months before the wedding. Allow an additional month for engraved invitations. Invitations are traditionally issued by the bride's parents; but if the groom's parents are assuming some of the wedding expenses, the invitations should be in their names also. Mail all invitations at the same time, six to eight weeks before the wedding.

Options: There are three types of invitations: traditional/ formal, contemporary, and informal. The traditional/ formal wedding invitation is white, soft cream, or ivory with raised black lettering. The printing is done on the top page of a double sheet of thick quality paper; the inside is left blank. The contemporary invitation is typically an individualized presentation that makes a statement about the bride and groom. Informal invitations are often printed on the front of a single, heavyweight card and may be handwritten or preprinted.

There are three types of printing: engraving, thermography, and offset printing. Engraving is the most expensive, traditional, and formal type of printing. It also takes the longest to complete. In engraved printing, stationery is pressed onto a copper plate, which makes the letters rise slightly from the page. Thermography is a process that fuses powder and ink to create a raised letter. This takes less time than engraving and is less expensive because copper plates do not have to be engraved. Offset printing, the least expensive, is the quickest to produce and offers a variety of styles and colors. It is also the least formal.

Things to Consider: If all your guests are to be invited to both the ceremony and the reception, a combined invitation may be sent without separate enclosure cards. Order one invitation for each married or cohabiting couple that you plan to invite. The officiant and his and her spouse, as well as your attendants, should receive an invitation.

Order approximately 20 percent more stationery than your actual count. Allow a minimum of two weeks to address and mail the invitations, longer if using a calligrapher or if your guest list is very large. You may also want to consider ordering invitations to the rehearsal dinner, as these should be in the same style as the wedding invitation.

SAMPLES OF TRADITIONAL/FORMAL INVITATIONS

1) When the bride's parents sponsor the wedding:

Mr. and Mrs. Alexander Waterman Smith
request the honor of your presence
at the marriage of their daughter
Carol Ann
to
Mr. William James Clark
on Saturday, the fifth of August
two thousand eight
at two o'clock in the afternoon
Saint James by-the-Sea
La Jolla, California

2) When the groom's parents sponsor the wedding:

Mr. and Mrs. Michael Burdell Clark
request the honor of your presence
at the marriage of
Miss Carol Ann Smith
to their son
Mr. William James Clark

3) When both the bride and groom's parents sponsor the wedding:

Mr. and Mrs. Alexander Waterman Smith
and
Mr. and Mrs. Michael Burdell Clark
request the honor of your presence
at the marriage of their children
Miss Carol Ann Smith
to
Mr. William James Clark

OR

Mr. and Mrs. Alexander Waterman Smith
request the honor of your presence
at the marriage of their daughter
Carol Ann Smith
to
William James Clark
son of Mr. and Mrs. Michael Burdell Clark

4) When the bride and groom sponsor their own wedding:

> The honor of your presence is requested
> at the marriage of
> Miss Carol Ann Smith
> and
> Mr. William James Clark

OR

> Miss Carol Ann Smith
> and
> Mr. William James Clark
> request the honor of your presence
> at their marriage

5) With divorced or deceased parents:

  a) When the bride's mother is sponsoring the wedding and is not remarried:

> Mrs. Julie Hurden Smith
> requests the honor of your presence
> at the marriage of her daughter
> Carol Ann

b) **When the bride's mother is sponsoring the wedding and has remarried:**
Mrs. Julie Hurden Booker
requests the honor of your presence
at the marriage of her daughter
Carol Ann Smith

OR

Mr. and Mrs. John Thomas Booker
request the honor of your presence
at the marriage of Mrs. Booker's daughter
Carol Ann Smith

c) **When the bride's father is sponsoring the wedding and has not remarried:**
Mr. Alexander Waterman Smith
requests the honor of your presence
at the marriage of his daughter
Carol Ann

d) **When the bride's father is sponsoring the wedding and has remarried:**
Mr. and Mrs. Alexander Waterman Smith
request the honor of your presence
at the marriage of Mr. Smith's daughter
Carol Ann

6) With deceased parents:
   a) When a close friend or relative sponsors the wedding:

   > Mr. and Mrs. Brandt Elliott Lawson
   > request the honor of your presence
   > at the marriage of their granddaughter
   > Carol Ann Smith

7) In military ceremonies, the rank determines the placement of names:
   a) Any title lower than sergeant should be omitted. Only the branch of service should be included under that person's name:

   > Mr. and Mrs. Alexander Waterman Smith
   > request the honor of your presence
   > at the marriage of their daughter
   > Carol Ann
   > to
   > William James Clark
   > United States Army

b) **Junior officers' titles are placed below their names and are followed by their branch of service:**

Mr. and Mrs. Alexander Waterman Smith
request the honor of your presence
at the marriage of their daughter
Carol Ann
to
William James Clark
First Lieutenant, United States Army

c) **If the rank is higher than lieutenant, titles are placed before names, and the branch of service is placed on the following line:**

Mr. and Mrs. Alexander Waterman Smith
request the honor of your presence
at the marriage of their daughter
Carol Ann
to
Captain William James Clark
United States Navy

SAMPLE OF A LESS FORMAL/MORE CONTEMPORARY INVITATION

Mr. and Mrs. Alexander Waterman Smith
would like you to

join with their daughter
Carol Ann
and
William James Clark
in the celebration of their marriage

For additional wording suggestions, log on to WedSpace.com.

Tips to Save Money: Thermography looks like engraving and is one-third the cost. Choose paper stock that is reasonable and yet achieves your overall look. Select invitations that can be mailed using just one stamp. Order at least 25 extra invitations in case you ruin some or add people to your list. To reorder this small number of invitations later would cost nearly three times the amount you'll spend up front.

Price Range: $0.75 - $6 per invitation

RESPONSE CARDS

Response cards are enclosed with the invitation to determine the number of people who will be attending your wedding. They are the smallest card size accepted by the postal service and should be printed in the same style as the invitation. An invitation to only the wedding ceremony does not usually include a request for a reply. However, response cards should be used when it is necessary to have an exact head count for special seating arrangements. Response cards are widely accepted today. If included, these cards should be easy for your guests to understand and use. Include a self-addressed and stamped return envelope to make it easy for your guests to return the response cards.

Things to Consider: You should not include a line that reads "number of persons" on your response cards because only those whose names appear on the inner and outer envelopes are invited. Each couple, each single person, and all children over the age of 16 should receive their own invitation. Indicate on the inner envelope if they may bring an escort or guest. The omitting of children's names from the inner envelope infers that the children are not invited.

Samples of wording for response cards:

M_____
(The M may be eliminated from the line, especially if many Drs. are invited)
___ accepts
___ regrets
Saturday the fifth of July
Oceanside Country Club

OR
The favor of your reply is requested
by the twenty-second of May
M_____
will _____ attend

Price Range: $0.40 - $1 each

RECEPTION CARDS

If the guest list for the ceremony is larger than that for the reception, a separate card with the date, time and location for the reception should be enclosed with the ceremony invitation for those guests also invited to the reception. Reception cards should be placed in front of the invitation, facing the back flap and the person inserting them. They should be printed on the same quality paper and in the same style as the invitation itself.

Sample of a formally worded reception card:

Mr. and Mrs. Alexander Waterman Smith
request the pleasure of your company
Saturday, the third of July
at three o'clock
Oceanside Country Club
2020 Waterview Lane
Oceanside, California

Sample of a less formal reception card:

Reception immediately following the ceremony
Oceanside Country Club
2020 Waterview Lane
Oceanside, California

Things to Consider: You may also include a reception card in all your invitations if the reception is to be held at a different site than the ceremony.

Tips to Save Money: If all people invited to the ceremony are also invited to the reception, include the reception information on the invitation and eliminate the reception card. This will save printing and postage costs.

Price Range: $0.40 - $1 each

CEREMONY CARDS

If the guest list for the reception is larger than the guest list for the ceremony, a special insertion card with the date, time, and location for the ceremony should be enclosed with the reception invitation for those guests also invited to the ceremony.

Ceremony cards should be placed in front of the invitation, facing the back flap and the person inserting them. They should be printed on the same quality paper and in the same style as the invitation itself.

Price Range: $0.40 - $1 each

ADDRESSING INVITATIONS

We recommend that you start addressing your invitations at least three months before your wedding, and preferably four months if your guest list is above 200 or if you are using a calligrapher.

Full instructions on addressing invitations appears in the groom's book, as this is one of many ways he can help with wedding planning.

You may also ask your bridesmaids or maid of honor to help, or, if you are working with a wedding consultant, he or she can also help you address invitations.

Whomever you ask, make a day of it — order takeout, pour a drink, or put on music. Focus on finishing the task at hand, but make it fun!

PEW CARDS

Pew cards may be used to let special guests and family members know they are to be seated in the reserved section on either the bride's side or the groom's side. These are most typically seen in large, formal ceremonies. Guests should take this card to the ceremony and show it to the ushers, who should then escort them to their seats.

Options: Pew cards may indicate a specific pew number if specific seats are assigned, or may read "Within the Ribbon" if certain pews are reserved, but no specific seat is assigned.

Things to Consider: Pew cards may be inserted along with the invitation, or may be sent separately after the RSVPs have been returned. It is often easier to send them after you have received all RSVPs so you know how many reserved pews will be needed.

Tips to Save Money: Include the pew card with the invitation to special guests and just say, "Within the Ribbon." After you have received all your RSVPs, you will know how many pews need to be reserved. This will save you the cost of mailing the pew cards separately.

Price Range: $0.25 - $1 each

SEATING/PLACE CARDS

Seating/place cards are used to let guests know where they should be seated at the reception and are a good way of putting people together so they feel most comfortable. Place cards should be laid out alphabetically on a table at the entrance to the reception. Each card should correspond to a table—either by number, color, or other identifying factor. Each table should be marked accordingly.

Options: Select a traditional or contemporary design for your place cards, depending on the style of your wedding. Regardless of the design, place cards must contain the same information: the bride and groom's names on the first line; the date on the second line; the third line is left blank for you to write in the guest's name; and the fourth line is for the table number, color, or other identifying factor.

Price Range: $0.25 - $1 each

RAIN CARDS

These cards are enclosed when guests are invited to an outdoor ceremony and/or reception, informing them of an alternate location in case of bad weather. As with other enclosures, rain cards should be placed in front of the invitation, facing the back flap and the person inserting them.

They should be printed on the same quality paper and in the same style as the invitation itself.

Price Range: $0.25 - $1 each

MAPS

Maps to the ceremony and/or reception are becoming frequent inserts in wedding invitations. They need to be drawn and printed in the same style as the invitation and are usually on a small, heavier card. If they are not printed in the same style or on the same type of paper as the invitation, they should be mailed separately.

Options: Maps should include both written and visual instructions, keeping in mind the fact that guests may be coming from different locations.

Things to Consider: Order extra maps to hand out at the ceremony if the reception is at a different location.

Tips to Save Money: If you are comfortable with computers, you can purchase software that allows you to draw your own maps. Print a map to both the ceremony and reception on the same sheet of paper, perhaps one on each side. This will save you the cost of mailing two maps. Or have your ushers hand out maps to the reception after the ceremony.

Price Range: $0.50 - $1 each

ANNOUNCEMENTS

Announcements are not obligatory but serve a useful purpose. They may be sent to friends who are not invited to the wedding because the number of guests must be limited or because they live too far away. They may also be sent to acquaintances who, while not particularly close to the family, might still wish to know about the marriage.

Announcements are also appropriate for friends and acquaintances who are not expected to attend and for whom you do not want to give an obligation of sending a gift. They should include the day, month, year, city, and state where the ceremony took place.

Things to Consider: Announcements should never be sent to anyone who has received an invitation to the wedding. They are printed on the same paper and in the same style as the invitation. They should be addressed before the wedding and mailed the day of or the day after the ceremony.

Price Range: $0.75 - $2 each

THANK-YOU NOTES

Regardless of whether the bride has thanked the donor in person or not, she must write a thank-you note for every gift received.

Things to Consider: Order thank-you notes along with your other stationery at least four months before your wedding. You should order some with your maiden initials for thank-you notes sent before the ceremony, and the rest with your married initials for notes sent after the wedding and for future use. Send thank-you notes within two weeks of receiving a gift that arrives before the wedding, and within two months after the honeymoon for gifts received on or after your wedding day. Be sure to mention the gift you received and let the person know how much you like it and what you plan to do with it.

Price Range: $0.40 - $0.75 each

STAMPS

Don't forget to budget stamps for response cards as well as for invitations!

Things to Consider: Don't order stamps until you have had the post office weigh your completed invitation.

It may exceed the size and weight for one stamp. Order commemorative stamps that fit the occasion.

Price Range: $0.39 - $1 per each invitation

CALLIGRAPHY

Calligraphy is a form of elegant handwriting often used to address invitations for formal occasions. Traditional wedding invitations should be addressed in black or blue fountain pen.

Options: You may address the invitations yourself, hire a professional calligrapher, or have your invitations addressed using calligraphy by computer. Make sure you use the same method or person to address both the inner and outer envelopes.

Tips to Save Money: You may want to consider taking a short course to learn the art of calligraphy so that you can address your own invitations. If you have a computer with a laser printer, you can address the invitations yourself using one of many beautiful calligraphy fonts.

Price Range: $0.50 - $3 each

NAPKINS/MATCHBOOKS

Napkins and matchbooks may also be ordered from and personalized by your stationer. These are placed around the reception room as decorative items and mementos of the event.

Things to Consider: Napkins and matchbooks can be printed in your wedding colors, or simply white with gold or silver lettering. You can include your names and wedding date or any special message.

Price Range: $0.50 - $1.50 each

CEREMONY PROGRAMS

Ceremony programs are printed documents showing the sequence of events during the ceremony. These programs add a personal touch to your wedding and are a convenient way of letting guests know who your attendants, officiant, and ceremony musicians are.

Options: Ceremony programs can be handed out by the ushers, or they can be placed at the back of the church for guests to take as they enter.

Price Range: $0.75 - $3 each

SAMPLE CEREMONY PROGRAM

The Marriage of
Carol Ann Smith and William James Clark
the eleventh of March
San Diego, California

OUR CEREMONY

Prelude:
All I Ask of You, by Andrew Lloyd Webber

Processional:
Canon in D Major, by Pachelbel

Rite of Marriage

Welcome guests

Statement of intentions

Marriage vows

Exchange of rings

Blessing of bride and groom

Pronouncement of marriage

Presentation of the bride and groom

Recessional:
Trumpet Voluntary, by Jeromiah Clarke

OUR WEDDING PARTY

Maid of Honor:
Susan Smith, Sister of Bride

Best Man:
Brandt Clark, Brother of Groom

Bridesmaids:
Janet Anderson, Friend of Bride
Lisa Bennett, Friend of Bride

Ushers:
Mark Gleason, Friend of Groom
Tommy Olson, Friend of Groom

Officiant:
Father Henry Thomas

OUR RECEPTION

Please join us after the ceremony
in the celebration of our marriage at:
La Valencia Hotel
1132 Prospect Street
La Jolla, California

RECEPTION

The reception is a party where all your guests come together to celebrate your new life as a married couple. It should reflect and complement the formality of your ceremony. The selection of a reception site will depend on its availability, price, proximity to the ceremony site, and the number of people it will accommodate.

RECEPTION SITE FEE

There are two basic types of reception sites. The first type charges a per-person fee that includes the facility, food, tables, silverware, china, and so forth. Examples: hotels, restaurants, and catered yachts. The second type charges a room rental fee and you are responsible for providing the food, beverages, linens, and possibly tables and chairs. Examples: clubs, halls, parks, museums, and private homes.

The advantage of the first type is that almost everything is done for you. The disadvantage, however, is that your choices of food, china, and linen are limited. Usually you are not permitted to bring in an outside caterer and must select from a predetermined menu.

Options: Private homes, gardens, hotels, clubs, restaurants, halls, parks, museums, yachts, and wineries are some of the more popular choices for receptions.

Things to Consider: When comparing the cost of different locations, consider the rental fee, food, beverages, parking, gratuity, setup charges, and the cost of rental equipment needed such as tables, chairs, canopies, and so forth.

Consider getting married on a Friday, Sunday or in the offseason, which is late October through February. Venues rent for much less on days other than Saturday evenings.

Be sure to get everything included in your price in writing and ask about extra, hidden fees. If your venue is a hotel ballroom, get the exact room in writing. Some hotels will reserve the right to move your wedding to a smaller room to accommodate another party.

If you are planning an outdoor reception, be sure to have a backup site in case of rain or rent a tent. If the price of a tent is out of your budget, see if there is another couple renting your venue that same weekend who is willing to share the cost with you.

Backyard weddings are very popular for couples with a

tight budget because it saves on a rental fee. If a close friend or family member will offer his or her home for your reception, this can be a money-saving option. However, be aware that having a backyard wedding isn't without its costs and caveats. You will need to consider how you will provide or rent tables, chairs, linens, place settings, lighting, a dance floor, parking (if the home doesn't have ample space for parking), restrooms (if the host doesn't want guests inside the home), and space for food prep, cooking and storage. You will also want to be sure the home is covered under the person's home owner's insurance, in case of an accident. If you do decide to have a backyard wedding however, it can be a memorable and personal reception venue.

Tips to Save Money: Since the cost of the reception is approximately 35% of the total cost of your wedding, you can save the most money by limiting your guest list. A sit-down dinner can easily cost $100 a head, so cutting just 10 people from your guest list could save $1,000.

Or, get creative and utilize a facility that is accessible to you for a low cost, such as your neighborhood's community center, country club's clubhouse, local library, public garden, local college or university, or zoo. If you think a venue has a nice ambiance, it doesn't hurt to inquire about hosting an event there.

Get a permit to have your wedding in a local park. Fees will probably be very low. Consider whether the venue provides ample seating, electrical outlets for your entertainment, restrooms, free parking, etc.

Price Range: $300 - $5,000

HORS D'OEUVRES

At receptions where a full meal is to be served, hors d'oeuvres may be offered to guests during the first hour of the reception. However, at a tea or cocktail reception, hors d'oeuvres will be the main course. Having an hors d'oeuvres-heavy cocktail hour, instead of a sit-down dinner, can save money on catering.

Options: There are many options for hors d'oeuvres, depending on the formality and theme of your reception. Popular items are foods that can easily be picked up and eaten with one hand. Hors d'oeuvres may be set out on tables "buffet style" for guests to help themselves, or they may be passed around on trays by waiters and waitresses.

Things to Consider: When selecting hors d'oeuvres for your reception, consider whether heating or refrigeration will be available and choose your food accordingly. When planning your menu, consider the time of day. You should select lighter hors d'oeuvres for a midday reception and heavier hors d'oeuvres for an evening reception.

Coordinate the food you serve with your theme and season; for instance, mini quesadillas and beef canapes for a Mexican fiesta-themed wedding or butternut squash soup shooters for a fall event.

Compare at least three caterers; there is a wide price range between caterers for the same food.

Tips to Save Money: Ask if you can take one of the hors d'oeuvres off the menu to lower the price.

Avoid serving hors d'oeuvres that are labor-intensive or that require expensive ingredients or cooling systems. For instance, skip the sushi bar.

Price Range: $3 - $20 per person

MAIN MEAL

If your reception is going to be at a hotel, restaurant or other facility that provides food, you will need to select a meal to serve your guests. Most of these facilities will have a predetermined menu from which to select your meal. If your reception is going to be in a facility that does not provide food, you will need to hire an outside caterer. The caterer will be responsible for preparing, cooking, and serving the food. The caterer will also be responsible for beverages and for cleaning up after the event. Before signing a contract, make sure you understand all the services the caterer will provide. Your contract should state the amount and type of food and beverages that will be served, the way in which they will be served, the number of servers who will be available, and the cost per food item or person.

Options: The main meal can be served either buffet style or as a sit-down meal. It should be chosen according to the time of day, year, and formality of the wedding. Although there are many main dishes to choose from, chicken and beef are the most popular selections for a large event. Ask your facility manager or caterer for their specialty. If you have a special type of food you would like to serve at your reception, select a facility or caterer who specializes in preparing it.

Things to Consider: When hiring a caterer, check to see if the location for your reception provides refrigeration and cooking equipment. If not, make sure your caterer is fully self-supported with portable refrigeration and heating equipment. Avoid mayonnaise, cream sauces, or custard fillings if food must go unrefrigerated for any length of time. A competent caterer will prepare much of the food in his or her own kitchen and should provide an adequate staff of cooks, servers, and bartenders.

Ask for references and look at photos from previous parties so you know how the food will be presented; or better yet, visit an event they are catering. A good caterer will set up a food tasting for you. Just be sure to doublecheck that the tasting is free. In some instances, caterers will try and charge for the tasting after the fact, if you don't book with them.

Tips to Save Money: Give only 85 to 95 percent of your final guest count to your caterer or facility manager. Oftentimes, a few guests who have RSVP'd won't show up. Additionally, caterers always provide extra food, in case of an emergency, so no one will go hungry. This is especially true with buffet-style receptions.

Consider a brunch or early afternoon wedding so the reception will fall between meals, allowing you to serve inexpensive breakfast food or hors d'oeuvres instead of a full meal.

Many weddings offer a trio of entree choices: typically, chicken, beef and fish. Serve only chicken to save about $20 a head, but make the dish special, with a citrus glaze or special sauce, for instance.

Price Range: $15 - $150 per person

SERVICE PROVIDERS' MEALS

Things to Consider: It is considered a courtesy to feed your photographer, videographer, and any other service provider at the reception. Check options and prices with your caterer or reception site manager. Make sure you allocate a place for your service providers to eat. You may want them to eat with your guests, or you may prefer setting a place outside the main room for them to eat. Your service providers may be more comfortable with the latter.

Tips to Save Money: You don't need to feed your service providers the same meal as your guests. You can order sandwiches or another less expensive meal for them. If the meal is a buffet, there should be enough food left after all your guests have been served for your service providers to eat. Tell them they are welcome to eat after all your guests have been served. Be sure to discuss this with your catering manager.

Price Range: $10 - $30 per person

PARTY FAVORS

Party favors are items given to your guests as mementos of your wedding. They are typically personalized with your names and wedding date or coordinate with your theme.

Options: Frames, candles, CDs of music, jams and jellies, flower seeds, chocolates, or fine candy are all popular wedding favors. Wine or champagne bottles marked with the bride and groom's names and wedding date on a personalized label are also popular. These come in different sizes and can be purchased by the case.

Things to Consider: Personalized favors need to be ordered several weeks in advance.

Tips to Save Money: If you didn't rent the vases, have guests take centerpieces or floral decorations home as gifts.

Burning your own CDs of your favorite music can be an inexpensive gift; however, consider the size of your guest list and copyright laws.

Price Range: $1 - $15 per person

ONLINE PHOTO ALBUM

Skip the disposable cameras; these days, most guests will bring their own digital cameras, which take much sharper, clearer photos than their cardboard counterparts, anyhow. Create an online photo album where guests can go to upload their digital photos for all to see.

Options: There are many websites that allow you to create an online, shareable photo gallery, including Flickr, Snapfish, Picasa and Photobucket. Standard space is free, or you can purchase increased storage space for just $5 to $25 per year. Create a URL, login and password for your wedding gallery. Then, hand out small cards with this information at your wedding, or email the information to all your guests after the wedding so everyone can upload the photos they took.

Price Range: $0 - $25

ROSE PETALS/RICE

Rose petals or rice are traditionally tossed over the bride and groom as they leave the church after the ceremony or when they leave the reception to symbolize happiness, beauty, and prosperity.

Options: Rose petals, rice, sparklers or confetti are often used. You may also want to use grass or flower seeds, which do not need to be cleaned up if tossed over a grassy area.

Things to Consider: Some venues do not allow rose petals, which can be slippery, or confetti, which needs to be cleaned up. Sparklers are also a popular option that look beautiful in photos, although some venues do not allow them because they could be a smoke or fire hazard. Ask about your venue's policy.

Price Range: $0.35 - $2 per person

GIFT ATTENDANT

The gift attendant is responsible for watching over your gifts during the reception so that no one walks away with them. This is necessary only if your reception is held in a public area such as a hotel or outside garden where strangers may be walking by. It is not proper to have a friend or family member take on this duty as s/he would not enjoy the reception. The gift attendant should also be responsible for transporting your gifts from the reception site to your car or bridal suite.

Tips to Save Money: Hire a young boy or girl from your neighborhood to watch over your gifts at the reception.

Price Range: $20 - $100

NOTES

CEREMONY & RECEPTION MUSIC

CEREMONY MUSIC

Ceremony music is the music played during the prelude, processional, ceremony, recessional, and postlude. Prelude music is played while guests are being seated, 15 to 30 minutes before the ceremony begins. Processional music is played as the wedding party enters the ceremony site. Recessional music is played as the wedding party leaves the ceremony site. Postlude music is played while the guests leave the ceremony site.

Options: The most traditional musical instrument for wedding ceremonies is the organ. But guitars, pianos, flutes, harps, and violins are also popular today.

Popular selections for a Christian wedding:
- Trumpet Voluntary by Purcell
- The Bridal Chorus by Wagner
- Wedding March by Mendelssohn
- Postlude in G Major by Handel

- Canon in D Major by Pachelbel
- Adagio in A Minor by Bach

Popular selections for a Jewish wedding:
- Erev Shel Shoshanim
- Erev Ba
- Hana' Ava Babanot

Things to Consider: Music may or may not be included as part of the ceremony site fee. Be sure to check with your ceremony site about restrictions pertaining to music and the availability of musical instruments for your use. Discuss the selection of ceremony music with your officiant and musicians. Make sure the musicians know how to play the selections you request.

When selecting ceremony music, keep in mind the formality of your wedding, your religious affiliation, and the length of the ceremony. Also consider the location and time of day. If the ceremony is outside where there may be other noises such as traffic, wind, or people's voices, or if a large number of guests will be attending your ceremony, consider having the music, your officiant, and your vows amplified. Make sure there are electrical outlets close to where the instruments will be set up.

Tips to Save Money: Hire student musicians from your local university or high school.

Ask a friend to sing or play at your ceremony; he or she will be honored.

If you're planning to hire a band for your reception, consider hiring a scaled-down version of the same band to play at your ceremony, such as a trio of flute, guitar, and vocals. This could enable you to negotiate a "package" price.

If you're planning to hire a DJ for your reception, consider hiring him or her to play pre-recorded music at your ceremony.

Price Range: $100 - $900

RECEPTION MUSIC

Music is a major part of your reception, and should be planned carefully. Music helps create the atmosphere of your wedding. Special songs will make your reception unique. When you select music for your reception, keep in mind the age and musical preference of your guests, your budget, and any restrictions that the reception site may have. Bands and musicians are typically more expensive than DJs.

Options: You need to find a reliable DJ, band, or combination of instruments and vocalists who will play the type of music you want and keep guests feeling upbeat all night. They should have experience performing at wedding receptions so they understand the flow of the event and can hopefully act as your master of ceremonies.

Things to Consider: If you want your musician to be your MC, make sure he or she has a complete timeline for your reception in order to announce the various events such as the toasts, first dance, and cutting of the cake.

If you need a large variety of music to satisfy all your guests, consider hiring a DJ. Make sure you give him or her a list of the songs you want played at your reception and the sequence in which you want them played. You may also want to provide a "Do Not Play" list of songs you don't want the DJ to play, even if they are requested.

If you choose a live band, consider watching your musicians perform at another event before booking their services. You should provide them with a few modern songs you would like at your reception and see if they are able to play them. You should also find out if you need to provide prerecorded music to play while the musicians take a break during the reception.

You should consider whether you want to hire a regular DJ or an entertainer — a DJ who can also provide things like disco dance lessons for the crowd or a light show. Some

DJs interact with the crowd much more than others. Decide which type of DJ you want.

Be sure to check with your reception venue about any music restrictions. Some venues located in residential areas, for instance, may have a rule that music has to be off by 10 p.m. Consider this when you choosing a venue, as well.

Tips to Save Money: A DJ is typically less expensive than a "live" musician. Some facilities have contracts with certain DJs, and you may be able to save money by hiring one of them.

When you hold your wedding can also help you save money on your reception music. DJs and bands may charge 10 to 20 percent more for a Saturday night wedding. Additionally, booking a DJ near the holidays or on New Year's Eve can nearly double the price!

Check the music department of local colleges and universities for names of student musicians and DJs. You may be able to hire a student for a fraction of the price of a professional musician or DJ.

Price Range: $500 - $5,000

NOTES

_____

_____

_____

_____

_____

_____

_____

_____

_____

_____

_____

_____

_____

_____

_____

_____

_____

_____

_____

_____

_____

_____

_____

_____

_____

_____

_____

_____

_____

_____

BAKERY

Wedding cakes may be ordered from a caterer or from a bakery. Some hotels and restaurants may also be able to provide a wedding cake; however, you will probably be better off ordering your cake from a bakery that specializes in wedding cakes.

WEDDING CAKE

Options: When ordering your cake, you will have to decide not only on a flavor, but also on a size, shape, and color. The most common flavors are chocolate, carrot, lemon, and vanilla cake. Add a filling to your cake, such as mousse, custard, ganache or a fruit filling.

You and your fiancé should meet with bakers who offer free cake tastings so you can choose the flavors, icings and fillings you like best. If you can't agree on one flavor, have tiers of different flavors.

Things to Consider: Icing types and toppings vary the price and look of the cake. Fondant provides a smooth, satiny look and doesn't need refrigeration, making it very popular, although it is one of the most expensive icings and the taste is not always great. Marzipan is a paste made from ground almonds and sugar, which is a better-tasting alternative to fondant. It can also be molded into flowers and other decorations. Ganache and buttercream are also popular icings that are lighter and taste great, although they melt easily and may not be the best choice for outdoor weddings. Sugar gum paste is another type of icing that your baker can use to create figurines, flowers, shapes, and more.

Price Range: $2 - $12 per piece

CAKE DELIVERY/SETUP FEE

This is the fee charged by bakers to deliver and set up your wedding cake at the reception site. It usually includes a deposit on the cake pillars and plate which will be refunded upon their return to the baker.

Tips to Save Money: Have a friend or family member get a quick lesson on how to set up your cake. Have them pick it up and set it up the day of your wedding, then have the florist decorate the cake and/or cake table with flowers and greenery.

Price Range: $40 - $100

CAKE-CUTTING FEE

Most reception sites and caterers charge a fee for each slice of cake they cut if the cake is brought in from an outside bakery. This fee will probably shock you. It is simply their way of enticing you to order the cake through them. Unfortunately, many caterers will not allow a member of your party to cut the cake.

Tips to Save Money: Many hotels and restaurants include a dessert in the cost of their meal packages. If you forego this dessert and substitute your cake as the dessert, they may be willing to waive the cake-cutting fee. Be sure to ask them.

Price Range: $0.75 - $2.50 per person

CAKE TOPPER

The bride's cake is often topped with some sort of decoration. Bells, love birds, a bridal couple, your initials or two wedding rings are popular choices and can be saved as mementos of your wedding day.

Things to Consider: Some porcelain and heavy cake toppers need to be anchored down into the cake. Talk to your baker once you choose your cake topper.

Tips to Save Money: Borrow a cake top from a friend or a family member as "something borrowed," an age-old wedding tradition.

Have your florist set aside a few large blooms to use as a cake topper.

Make your own cake topper! This can be a fun, quick DIY project that can be redone as many times as needed until you get it right. Peruse an arts and crafts store to get ideas and buy supplies, such as styrofoam, wooden doll bodies, paint, and more.

Price Range: $10 - $150

CAKE KNIFE/TOASTING GLASSES

Your cake knife and toasting glasses can be rented, purchased or borrowed. The bride uses the cake knife to cut the first two slices of the wedding cake with the groom's hand placed over hers. The groom feeds the bride first. Then the bride feeds the groom.

You will use toasting glasses to toast each other after cutting the cake. They are usually decorated with ribbons or flowers and kept near the cake. This tradition makes beautiful wedding photographs.

Things to Consider: Consider having your initials and wedding date engraved on your wedding knife as a memento. Consider purchasing crystal or silver toasting glasses as a keepsake of your wedding.

Tips to Save Money: Borrow your cake knife or toasting glasses from a friend or family member.

Use the reception facility's glasses and knife, and decorate them with flowers or ribbon.

Purchasing a cake knife and glass set from a bridal retailer will be much more expensive than using a regular set of champagne flutes and a cake cutting set. Look for pretty items on sale at home stores or gift stores.

Price Range: $15 - $120 for knife; $10 - $100 for toasting glasses

NOTES

FLOWERS

Flowers add beauty, fragrance, and color to your wedding. A breathtaking bouquet or unique floral centerpiece gives your wedding a special style and romance. You may also want to use flowers or ribbons to mark the aisle pews and add color.

BRIDE'S BOUQUET

The bridal bouquet is one of the most important elements of the bride's attire and deserves special attention. Start by selecting the color and shape of the bouquet. The bridal bouquet should be carried low enough so that all the intricate details of your gown are visible.

Options: There are many colors, scents, sizes, shapes, and styles of bouquets to choose from. Popular styles are the cascade, cluster, posy, contemporary, waterfall, and hand-tied bouquets.

FLOWERS

The traditional bridal bouquet is made of white flowers. Stephanotis, gardenias, white roses, orchids, and lilies of the valley are popular choices for an all-white bouquet.

If you prefer a colorful bouquet, you may want to consider using roses, tulips, stock, peonies, freesia, and gerbera, which come in a wide variety of colors. Using scented flowers in your bouquet will evoke memories of your wedding day whenever you smell them in the future. Popular fragrant flowers are gardenias, freesia, stephanotis, bouvardia, and narcissus.

Some flowers carry centuries of symbolism. Consider stephanotis — tradition regards it as the bridal good-luck flower! Pimpernel signifies change; white flowers radiate innocence; forget-me-nots indicate true love; and ivy stands for friendship, fidelity, and matrimony — the three essentials for a happy marriage.

No flower, however, has as much symbolism for brides as the orange blossom, having at least 700 years of nuptial history. Its unusual ability to simultaneously bear flowers and produce fruit symbolizes the fusion of beauty, personality, and fertility.

Things to Consider: Your flowers should complement the season, your gown, your color scheme, your attendants' attire, and the style and formality of your wedding. When you visit your florist, bring a photo or description of your dress and your wedding party's attire. You don't want an elaborate bouquet to overwhelm you; likewise, you don't want a small bouquet to get lost next to a ballgown. Typically, the bigger the dress, the bigger the bouquet.

Whatever flowers you select, final arrangements should be made well in advance of your wedding date to ensure availability. Confirm your final order and delivery time a few days before the wedding. Have the flowers delivered before the photographer arrives so that you can include them in your pre-ceremony photos.

In determining the size of your bouquet, consider your gown and your overall stature. Carry a smaller bouquet if you're petite or if your gown is fairly ornate. A long, cascading bouquet complements a fairly simple gown or a tall or larger bride. Arm bouquets look best when resting naturally in the crook of your arm. For a natural, fresh-picked look, have your florist put together a cluster of flowers tied together with a ribbon. For a Victorian appeal, carry a nosegay or a basket filled with flowers. Or carry a Bible or other family heirloom decorated with just a few flowers. For a contemporary look, you may want to consider carrying an arrangement of calla lilies or other long-stemmed flower over your arm. For a dramatic statement, carry a single stem of your favorite flower!

If your bouquet includes delicate flowers that will not withstand hours of heat or a lack of water, make sure your florist uses a bouquet holder to keep them fresh. If you want to carry fresh-cut stems without a bouquet holder, make sure the flowers you select are hardy enough to go without water for the duration of your ceremony and reception.

Tips to Save Money: Avoid exotic or out-of-season flowers that will need to be shipped in from a distant location — the cost will be significantly higher. Select flowers that are in bloom and plentiful in your area at the time of your wedding.

Allow your florist to emphasize your colors using more reasonable, seasonal flowers to achieve your overall look. If you have a favorite flower that is costly or out of season, consider using silk for that one flower.

Use a few stems of a larger flower, such as hydrangea, peonies, or gerbera, rather than buying more stems of a smaller flower.

Pad your bouquet to make it look more full, using baby's breath, ivy, eucalyptus, succulents and more. A good florist will know tricks for making a few flowers go a long way.

Avoid labor-intensive designs, such as cascade and waterfall bouquets. Also, flowers that require wiring or floral taping, such as orchids, sweet peas, and other delicate flowers, will cost more than thick, long-stemmed flowers like gerbera, roses and carnations.

Avoid scheduling your wedding near holidays such as Valentine's Day and Mother's Day when the price of flowers is higher.

Price Range: $25 - $400

MAID OF HONOR & BRIDESMAIDS' BOUQUETS

Choose a bouquet style for your attendants that complements the formality of your wedding and their dresses. The maid of honor's bouquet can be somewhat larger or of a different color than the rest of the bridesmaids' bouquets. This will help to set her apart from the others. The bridesmaids' bouquets should complement the bridal bouquet, but are generally smaller in size.

Options: Bridesmaids' bouquets can be identical or can each be a different flower that make up the bridal bouquet.

Things to Consider: If your bridesmaids will be wearing floral print dresses, select flowers that subtly complement the floral print.

Tips to Save Money: Have your attendants carry a single stemmed rose, lily, or other long-stemmed flower for an elegant look that also saves money.

Using a single type of flower for all the bridesmaids' bouquets can save money. Or, ask for a posy bouquet, a smaller version of a nosegay, which is a tight cluster of flowers. Then have your attendants decorate the cake table or other area of the reception with their bouquets.

Price Range: $25 - $100

MAID OF HONOR & BRIDESMAIDS' HAIRPIECES

You may want your maid of honor and bridesmaids to wear flowers in their hair, especially for an outdoor or garden wedding.

Things to Consider: If you use real flowers in the hairpiece, they must be hardy and able to withstand the heat.

Tips to Save Money: Consider using artificial flowers for the hairpieces as long as they are in keeping with the flowers carried in bouquets. A simply DIY project can be to purchase silk flowers from a crafts store, remove the stems, and hot glue the bloom to a hair clip or headband.

Price Range: $8 - $100

FLOWER GIRL'S HAIRPIECE

Flower girls often wear a wreath of flowers as a hairpiece.

Options: This is another place where artificial flowers may be used, but they must be in keeping with the flowers carried by members of the bridal party.

Things to Consider: Be sure to give your florist your flower girl's head measurements so the wreath is the correct size. If the flowers used are not a sturdy and long-lived variety, a ribbon or bow might be a safer choice.

Price Range: $8 - $75

BRIDE'S GOING AWAY CORSAGE

Traditionally, couples would leave right from their weddings to go on their honeymoons; thus, changed into a going away outfit, complete with floral corsage.

Tips to Save Money: Ask your florist if he or she can design your bridal bouquet in such a way that the center flowers may be removed and worn as a corsage. Or omit this corsage altogether.

Price Range: $10 - $50

TOSSING BOUQUET

Tradition has it that the single woman who catches the bouquet is the next to be married. If you want to preserve your bridal bouquet during the bouquet toss, consider having your florist make a smaller, less expensive bouquet specifically for tossing.

Tips to Save Money: Use the floral cake top or guest book table "tickler bouquet" as the tossing bouquet. Or omit the tossing bouquet altogether and simply toss your bridal bouquet.

Price Range: $20 - $100

MAIN ALTAR

The purpose of flowers at the main altar is to direct the guests' visual attention toward the front of the church or synagogue and to the bridal couple. Your officiant's advice, or that of the altar guild or florist, can be most helpful in choosing flowers for the altar.

Options: If your ceremony is outside, decorate the arch, gazebo, or other structure serving as the altar with flowers or greenery. In a Jewish ceremony, vows are said under a Chuppah, which is placed at the altar and covered with greens and fresh flowers.

Things to Consider: In choosing floral accents, consider the decor of your ceremony site. Some churches and synagogues are ornate enough and don't need extra flowers. Too many arrangements would get lost in the architectural splendor. Select a few dramatic showpieces that will complement the existing decor. Be sure to ask if there are any restrictions on flowers at the church or synagogue. Remember, decorations should be determined by the size and style of the building, the formality of the wedding, the preferences of the bride, the cost, and the regulations of the particular site.

Tips to Save Money: Choose a ceremony site that is already beautiful and elegant. For instance, many outdoor venues won't need flowers, or a church with candlelight and stained glass windows may not need extra decorations.

Your ceremony site may have decorations you can use free of charge, especially things like poinsettias and candles around the holidays. Be sure to ask.

Reuse the main altar floral decorations at your reception site. Just consider the cost of transportation and setup at both locations.

Price Range: $50 - $3,000

AISLE PEWS

Flowers, candles, or ribbons are often used to mark the aisle pews and add color.

Options: A cluster of flowers, a cascade of greens, or a cascade of flowers and ribbons are all popular choices.

Things to Consider: Use hardy flowers that can tolerate being handled as pew ornaments. Gardenias and camellias, for example, are too sensitive to last long. Avoid using allium in your aisle pew decorations as they have an odor of onions.

Tips to Save Money: It is not necessary to decorate all of the aisle pews, or any at all. To save money, decorate only the reserved family pews. Or decorate every second or third pew.

Consider a non-floral element to save money. Mason jars with tea lights or large seashells hung from ribbons can be lovely along the aisle.

Price Range: $5 - $75

RECEPTION SITE

Flowers add beauty, fragrance, and color to your reception. Flowers for the reception, like everything else, should fit your overall style and color scheme. Flowers can help transform a stark reception hall into a warm, inviting, and colorful room.

Things to Consider: You can rent indoor plants or small trees to give your indoor reception a garden-like atmosphere. Decorate them with strands of inexpensive lights.

Tips to Save Money: You can save money by taking flowers from the ceremony to the reception site for decorations. However, you must coordinate this move carefully to avoid having your guests arrive at an undecorated reception room. Use greenery rather than flowers to fill large areas. Trees and garlands of ivy can give a dramatic impact for little money.

Or, have your reception outside in a beautiful garden or by the water, surrounded by nature's own beauty and use only small table decorations.

Price Range: $300 - $3,000

HEAD TABLE

The head table is where the wedding party will sit during the reception. This important table should be decorated with a larger or more dramatic centerpiece than the guest tables.

Tips to Save Money: Decorate the head table with the bridal and attendants' bouquets.

Use small, short table centerpieces, which are much less expensive than tall ones.

Price Range: $100 - $600

TABLE CENTERPIECES

Each of the guests tables at your reception should be decorated with a centerpiece.

Options: Candles, mirrors, water centerpieces and flowers are popular choices for table centerpieces. However, the options are endless. Just be creative! An arrangement of shells, for example, makes a very nice centerpiece for a seaside reception. Floating candles in a low, round bowl make a romantic centerpiece for an evening reception.

Tips to Save Money: Use small potted flowering plants or succulents. After the reception, you can give them as gifts.

Instead of flowers, use inexpensive themed decorations as centerpieces instead. Consider paper lanterns and take-out boxes to create Asian-inspired style. Or, consider decorations that represent you as a couple; for instance, a pair of writers might decorate with vintage books.

Shop at antique stores and on eBay for vintage pieces like mason jars, milk crates, vases, and glass bowls, which can be filled with flowers, stones, or buttons for inexpensive, pretty centerpieces.

Mix non-floral natural elements with flowers to cut back on your flower order. Stones, fruit, shells, and succulents make for a unique, modern look when mixed with a few flowers.

Candles give the room a warm, romantic glow and can be bought cheaply, in bulk.

Things to Consider: The arrangements should complement the table linens and the size of the table, and should be kept low enough so as not to hinder conversation among guests seated across from each other. Consider using a centerpiece that your guests can take home as a memento of your wedding.

FLOWERS

Avoid using highly fragrant flowers, like narcissus, on tables where food is being served or eaten.

Price Range: $100 - $1,000

BUFFET TABLE

If buffet tables are used, have some type of floral arrangement on the tables to add color and beauty to your display of food.

Things to Consider: Avoid placing certain flowers, such as carnations, snapdragons, or the star of Bethlehem, next to buffet displays of fruits or vegetables, as they are extremely sensitive to the gasses emitted by these foods and may wilt.

Tips to Save Money: Instead of flowers, opt for whole fruits and bunches of berries. Figs add a festive touch. Pineapples are a sign of hospitality. Vegetables offer an endless array of options to decorate with.

Decorate with fragrant herbs used in the food you are serving, such as basil, rosemary, mint and more.

Price Range: $50 - $300

CAKE TABLE

The wedding cake is often the central focal point at the reception. Decorate the cake table with flowers.

Tips to Save Money: Have your bridesmaids place their bouquets on the cake table during the reception.

Decorate the cake top only and surround the base of the cake with greenery and a few loose flowers.

Price Range: $30 - $300

CAKE

Flowers are a beautiful addition to a wedding cake and are commonly seen as a cake topper or spilling out between the cake tiers.

Things to Consider: Use only nonpoisonous flowers, and have your florist — not the caterer — design the floral decorations for your cake. A florist will be able to blend the cake decorations into your overall floral theme.

Tips to Save Money: Use just a few large, beautiful blooms instead of numerous smaller flowers.

FLOWERS

Have your baker design realistic-looking flowers out of fondant or sugar paste instead of using real flowers.

Price Range: $20 - $100

FLORAL DELIVERY/SETUP

Most florists charge a fee to deliver flowers to the ceremony and reception sites and to arrange them onsite.

Things to Consider: Make sure your florist knows where your sites are and what time to arrive for setup.

Tips to Save Money: If you're having a small wedding or a wedding with very few floral decorations, purchase your own flowers wholesale and ask family and friends to help you set them up.

Price Range: $25 - $200

FLOWERS AND THEIR SEASONS

SUMMER

Allium

Amaryllis

Billy Buttons

Celosia

Dahlia

Delphinium

Liatris

Lisianthus

Pincushion

Queen Anne's Lace

Saponaria

Snapdragon

Speedwell

Sunflower

Tuberose

FALL

Amaryllis

Anemones

Dahlia

Delphinium

Liatris

Lisianthus

Narcissus

Protea

Snapdragon

Star of Bethlehem

Tuberose

WINTER

Amaryllis

Anemones

Narcissus

Protea

Star of Bethlehem

Tulip

Waxflower

FLOWERS AND THEIR SEASONS (CONT.)

SPRING	YEAR-ROUND
Allium	Alstroemeria
Anemones	Aster
Billy Buttons	Baby's Breath
Celosia	Bachelor's Button
Daffodils	Bird of Paradise
Liatris	Bouvardia
Lily of the Valley	Calla Lily
Lisianthus	Carnation
Narcissus	Chrysanthemum
Peony	Eucalyptus
Ranunculus	Freesia
Snapdragon	Gardenia
Sunflower	Gerbera
Sweet Pea	Gladiolus
Tulip	Iris
Waxflower	Lily
	Nerine
	Orchid
	Rose
	Statice
	Stephanotis
	Stock

RENTAL ITEMS

Not all items for the ceremony and reception need to be purchased. There are many items that you have the option of renting, such as a tent, chairs, and linens. Rentals also allow you to host a reception in your own home or in less traditional locations, such as an art museum, a local park, or at the beach. Be sure to take into account the cost for all these rental items when creating your budget.

CEREMONY ACCESSORIES

Ceremony rental accessories are the additional items needed for the ceremony but not included in the ceremony site fee. Ceremony rental accessories may include the following items:

Aisle Runner: A thin rug made of plastic, paper or cloth extending the length of the aisle. It is rolled out after the mothers are seated, just prior to the processional. Plastic or paper doesn't work well on grass; but if you must use one of these types of runners, make sure the grass is clipped short.

Kneeling Cushion: A small cushion or pillow placed in front of the altar where the bride and groom kneel for their wedding blessing.

Arch (Christian): A white lattice or brass arch where the bride and groom exchange their vows, often decorated with flowers and greenery.

Chuppah (Jewish): A canopy under which a Jewish ceremony is performed, symbolizing cohabitation and consummation.

You may also need to consider renting audio equipment, aisle stanchions, candelabra, candles, candle-lighters, chairs, heaters, a gift table, a guest book stand, and a canopy.

Things to Consider: Make sure the rental supplier has been in business for a good amount of time and has a good reputation. Reserve the items you need well in advance. Find out the company's payment, reservation, and cancellation policies.

Some companies allow you to reserve emergency items, such as heaters or canopies, without having to pay for them unless needed, in which case you would need to call the rental company a day or two in advance to request the items. If someone else requests the items you have reserved, the company should give you the right of first refusal.

Tips to Save Money: Negotiate a package deal, if possible, by renting items for both the ceremony and the reception from the same supplier. Consider renting these items from your florist so you only have to pay one delivery fee.

Price Range: $100 - $500

TENT/CANOPY

A large tent or canopy may be required for receptions held outdoors to protect you and your guests from the sun or rain. Tents and canopies can be expensive due to the labor involved in delivery and setup.

Options: Tents and canopies come in different sizes and shapes and with different amenities. Some have side flaps, heaters and cooling, and flooring for a lawn reception. Contact several party rental suppliers to discuss the options.

Things to Consider: Consider this cost when making a decision between an outdoor and an indoor reception. Be aware of whether you will need heating or cooling inside the tent, as well.

Tips to Save Money: Shop early and compare prices with several party rental suppliers. If there is another couple hosting a wedding at your same venue during the same weekend, contact them about splitting the cost of a tent.

Price Range: $300 - $5,000

DANCE FLOOR

A dance floor will be provided by most hotels and clubs. However, if your reception site does not have a dance floor, you may need to rent one through your caterer or a party rental supplier.

Things to Consider: When comparing prices of dance floors, include the delivery and setup fees.

Price Range: $100 - $600

TABLES/CHAIRS

You will have to provide tables and chairs for your guests if your reception site or caterer doesn't provide them as part of their package. For a full meal, you will have to provide tables and seating for all guests. For a cocktail reception, you only need to provide tables and chairs for approximately 30 to 50 percent of your guests. Ask your caterer or reception site manager for advice.

Options: There are various types of tables and chairs to choose from. The most commonly used chairs for wedding receptions are white wooden or plastic chairs. The most common tables for receptions are round tables that seat eight guests. The most common head table arrangement is several rectangular tables placed end-to-end to seat your entire wedding party on one side, facing your guests. Contact various party rental suppliers to find out what types of chairs and tables they carry, as well as their price ranges.

Things to Consider: When comparing prices of renting tables and chairs, include the cost of delivery and setup.

Tips to Save Money: Attempt to negotiate free delivery and setup with party rental suppliers in exchange for giving them your business.

Price Range: $3 - $10 per person

LINENS/TABLEWARE

You will also need to provide linens and tableware for your

reception if your reception site or caterer does not provide them as part of their package.

Options: For a sit-down reception where the meal is served by waiters and waitresses, tables are usually set with a cloth (usually white, but may be color coordinated with the wedding), a centerpiece, and complete place settings. At a less formal buffet reception where guests serve themselves, tables are covered with a cloth, but place settings are not mandatory. The necessary plates and silverware may be located at the buffet table, next to the food.

Things to Consider: Linens and tableware depend on the formality of your reception. When comparing prices of linens and tableware, include the cost of delivery and setup.

Tips to Save Money: It pays to shop around — your caterer may rent linens and tableware, but for a much higher price than an online retailer. Or, depending on the size of your wedding, it may actually be more cost-effective to purchase a set of tableware and resell it after the wedding.

Items like colored napkins and colored glassware will raise your rental costs. Stick to neutrals and save.

Price Range: $3 - $25 per person

HEATERS

You may need to rent heaters if your ceremony or reception will be held outdoors and if the temperature could drop below 65 degrees.

Options: There are electric and gas heaters, both of which come in different sizes. Gas heaters are more popular since they do not have unsightly and unsafe electric cords.

Price Range: $25 - $75 each

LANTERNS

Lanterns are often used at evening receptions to add soft lighting.

Options: Many choices are available, from fire lanterns to electric ones.

Tips to Save Money: For inexpensive paper lanterns that cost less than $1 each, try OrientalTrading.com.

Price Range: $12 - $60

MISCELLANEOUS RENTAL ITEMS

If your reception site or caterer doesn't provide them, you will need to purchase, rent, or borrow other miscellaneous items for your reception, such as trash cans, a gift table, trash bags, and so on.

GIFTS

Gifts are a wonderful way to show your appreciation to family, friends, members of your wedding party and to all those who have assisted you in your wedding planning process. Brides and grooms usually like to exchange something small yet meaningful. Keepsake items make wonderful gifts for members of the wedding party.

GROOM'S GIFT

The groom's gift is traditionally given by the bride to the groom.

Options: A watch, cufflinks, a set of golf clubs, electronics, or a beautiful album of boudoir photos are nice gifts.

Tips to Save Money: A letter from the bride proclaiming her love for the groom is a special, yet inexpensive gift.

Price Range: $50 - $500

BRIDESMAIDS' GIFTS

Bridesmaids' gifts are given by the bride to her bridesmaids and maid of honor as a permanent keepsake of the wedding.

Options: The perfect gift is jewelry or an accessory that can be worn both during and after the wedding. Choose earrings, a pashmina wrap, small clutch purse, or a hairpiece that complements your bridesmaids' dresses.

Other nice gift choices are a certificate for a spa treatment, personalized sweat suits or tank tops, favorite beauty products, a tote or cosmetic bag, and customized stationery.

Things to Consider: Bridesmaids' gifts are usually presented at the bridesmaids' luncheon, if there is one, or at the rehearsal dinner. The gift to the maid of honor may be similar to the bridesmaids' gifts, but should be a bit more expensive.

Tips to Save Money: Make bridesmaids a handmade gift, such as a hairpiece, earrings or other fun DIY project. Shop for deeply discounted gifts, such as pashminas and jewelry on sites like Overstock.com.

Consider buying the bridesmaids' dresses as your gift to your wedding party.

Price Range: $25 - $200 per gift

PARTIES

Weddings are often much more than a day-long celebration. Some traditional events include the engagement party, bridal shower, bachelor and bachelorette parties, bridesmaids' luncheon, and rehearsal dinner. Some couples also like to have a brunch the day after the wedding to relax and relive the previous evening's celebration. You should include whatever celebrations fall within your budget.

BRIDAL SHOWER

Traditionally, your wedding shower is thrown by your maid of honor and bridesmaids, unless they are a member of your immediate family. Because a shower is a gift-giving occasion, it is not considered socially acceptable for anyone in your immediate family to host this event. If your mother or sisters wish to be involved, have them offer to help with the cost of the event or offer their home for it. The agenda usually includes some games and gift-opening. Be sure to have someone keep track of which gift is from whom.

Options: Tea parties, spa days, cocktail parties, and traditional at-home events are all options — these days even men are being invited as coed showers become more and more popular! Generally, an event is themed (lingerie, cooking, home decor), and the invitation should give guests an idea of what type of gift to bring.

Things to Consider: You may have several showers thrown for you. When creating your guest lists, be sure not to invite the same people to multiple showers (the exception being members of the wedding party, who may be invited to all showers without the obligation of bringing a gift.) Only include people who have been invited to the wedding — the only exception to this is a work shower, to which all coworkers may be invited, whether or not they are attending the wedding.

BACHELORETTE PARTY

The bachelorette party is typically organized by the maid of honor for the females in the wedding party and any close family.

Options: Go out for dinner and drinks, have a spa day, go wine tasting or on a day-cruise. Other fun options include a yoga or Pilates retreat, scavenger hunt, or a sporting event.

Things to Consider: The maid of honor should ask the bride what kind of party she wants — wild or mild. She should not plan the party for the night before the wedding, as you don't want to have a hangover or be exhausted during your wedding. A few weeks before or another date when the whole party can get together is more appropriate for the bachelorette party. You should also coordinate transportation for guests who are drinking.

The maid of honor should consider buying something funny or unique for the bride to wear to make her stand out, such as a feather boa, tiara, or beads.

Tips to Save Money: Consider having the bachelorette party in the same city as the wedding, in the days leading up to the wedding. Opt for something less expensive, such as a day at the nail salon chatting and bonding with friends.

BRIDESMAIDS' LUNCHEON

The bridesmaids' luncheon is given by the bride for her bridesmaids. It is not a shower; rather, it is simply a time for good friends to get together formally before the bride changes her status from single to married.

Things to Consider: You can give your bridesmaids their gifts at this gathering. Otherwise, plan to give them their gifts at the rehearsal dinner.

Price Range: $12 - $60 per person

DAY-AFTER WEDDING BRUNCH

Many times, the newlyweds will want to host a brunch the day after the wedding to spend one last bit of time with their guests and to thank them for coming to the wedding. Brunch can be much less formal than the rest of the wedding.

Options: You can have your caterer provide food for this event. If many guests are at one hotel, consider having the brunch there. If the hotel offers a continental breakfast, ask the hotel to reserve space in the breakfast room for your group.

Things to Consider: Choose a reasonable time for the brunch: Not too early, as many guests will be recovering from the festivities of the reception, but not too late, as out-of-town guests will have travel arrangements to attend to.

Tips to Save Money: Enlist family members to help cook or pick up brunch foods. A family member who still wants to contribute to your wedding is a perfect choice to host. Keep the menu simple and have bagels, croissants, jam, fruit, coffee, and juice.

Price Range: $10 - $25 per person

WEDDING TRADITIONS

Have you ever wondered why certain things are almost always done at weddings? For example, why does the bride carry a bouquet or wear a veil? Or why do guests throw rice or rose petals over the newlyweds? In this section we discuss the origin and symbolism of some of the most popular wedding traditions.

THE BRIDE'S BOUQUET

In history, a bride carried her bouquet for protective reasons — carrying strong-smelling spices or garlic could help to drive away evil spirits which might plague the wedding. Eventually the floral bouquet became prevalent and symbolized fertility and the hope for a large family. Each flower was assigned a particular meaning when carried in a bride's bouquet.

THE BRIDE'S VEIL

The veil has historically symbolized virginity and innocence. It is believed that, in ancient times, a bride was veiled to protect her from evil spirits or to shield her from her husband's eyes. Arranged marriages were common and often they were not to officially meet until after the wedding.

RICE AND PETALS

The tossing of rice began to aid with fertility, both for the couple and for their harvest.

SOMETHING OLD, SOMETHING NEW, SOMETHING BORROWED, SOMETHING BLUE

Something old is carried to represent the history of the bride and ties her to her family. Something new represents the future and the bride's ties to her new family. Something borrowed should come from someone who is happily married and is carried in the hopes that their good fortune may rub off on you. Blue is the color of purity and is carried to represent faithfulness in the marriage. Many people don't realize that there is one more item — a sixpence in your shoe — which represents wealth.

WHITE AISLE RUNNER

Using a white aisle runner symbolizes bringing God into your union and is indicative of walking on holy ground.

SPECIAL SEATING FOR THE FAMILIES

The families are traditionally seated on opposite sides of the church, because in ancient times families would often have a wedding in order to bring peace to warring clans. In order to prevent fighting from taking place during the wedding, they were kept separate.

THE GROOM ENTERING FIRST

Traditionally, the groom enters first and gives his vows first, because he is considered to be the one who has initiated the wedding.

THE FATHER OF THE BRIDE WALKING DOWN THE AISLE

In historic times, brides were literally given away by their fathers — women were betrothed, often at birth, to men they did not know, and their parents were able to "give them away." Now, giving the bride away is simply a way for the bride's family to publicly show their support of the union.

THE BRIDE STANDING ON THE LEFT

Because ancient times were so violent and unpredictable, a bride was likely to be kidnapped and held for ransom at her wedding! The bride was placed on the groom's left in order to leave his sword-hand free in case he had to defend her.

THE SYMBOLISM OF THE WEDDING RINGS

The circle of the wedding ring represents eternal love and devotion. The Greeks believed that the fourth finger on the left hand has a vein which leads directly to the heart, so this is the finger onto which we place these bands.

KISSING THE BRIDE

During the Roman empire, the kiss between a couple symbolized a legal bond—hence the expression "sealed with a kiss." Continued use of the kiss to seal the marriage bond is based on the deeply rooted idea of the kiss as a vehicle for transference of power and souls.

THE COUPLE BEING PRONOUNCED "HUSBAND AND WIFE"

This establishes their change of names and a definite point in time for the beginning of the marriage. These words are to remove any doubt in the minds of the couple or the witnesses concerning the validity of the marriage.

SIGNING THE WEDDING PAPERS

The newlywed couple signs the wedding papers to establish a public document and a continuing public record of the covenant.

SIGNING THE GUEST BOOK

Your wedding guests are official witnesses to the covenant. By signing the guest book, they are saying, "I have witnessed the vows, and I will testify to the reality of this marriage." Because of this significance, the guest book should be signed after the wedding rather than before it.

THE PURPOSE OF THE RECEIVING LINE

The receiving line is for guests to give their blessings to the couple and their parents.

THE BRIDE AND GROOM FEEDING WEDDING CAKE TO EACH OTHER

This represents the sharing of their body to become one. A New Testament illustration of this symbolism is The Lord's Supper.

DO'S & DON'TS

Your wedding will last only a few hours but will likely take several months to plan. That is why it is so important to enjoy the complete wedding planning process. This is a time to get excited, to fall even more deeply in love with each other, to learn more about each other, and how to give and take. If you can handle your wedding planning with your fiancé and parents, you can handle anything! Here is a list of do's and don'ts when planning your special day. If you follow these suggestions, your wedding planning will be more enjoyable and the wedding itself will be much more smooth and beautiful.

DO'S

- Maintain open communication with your fiancé and with both sets of parents, especially if they are financing the wedding.

- Consult a professional wedding planner.

DO'S & DON'TS

- Maintain a sense of humor.

- Be receptive to your parents' ideas, especially if they are financing the wedding.

- Be flexible and keep your overall budget in mind.

- Choose a gown that will look beautiful but will allow you to dance, eat and enjoy your event.

- Buy *Wedding Party Responsibility Cards*, published by WS Publishing Group, and give a card to each member of your wedding party.

- Register for gifts; consider a price range that your guests can afford.

- Break in your shoes well before your wedding day.

- Practice with makeup and various hairstyles for your wedding day if you are doing hair and makeup yourself.

- Check recent references for all of your service providers.

- Get everything in writing with your service providers.

- Assign your guests to tables and group them together by age, interests, acquaintances, etc.

- Consider drawing up a prenuptial agreement and a will.

- Send thank-you notes as soon as you receive gifts.

- Give a rose to each of your mothers as you walk down the aisle during the recessional.

- Schedule yourself enough time for hair and makeup before the wedding so you won't be rushed.

- Try to spend some time with each of your guests and personally thank them for coming to your wedding.

- Encourage the bride's parents to introduce their family and friends to the family and friends of the groom's family, and vice versa.

- Toast both sets of parents at the rehearsal dinner and/or at the reception. Thank them for everything they have done for you and for giving you a beautiful wedding.

- Consider taking some photos before the ceremony so guests aren't kept waiting for a long time afterward. First Look photos are becoming very popular.

- Eat well at the reception. If you don't have much time, ask your caterer or wedding planner to set aside a plate for you and your fiancé.

DO'S & DON'TS

- Keep a smile on your face; there will be many photographs taken of both of you.

- Expect things to go wrong on your wedding day. Relax and don't let things bother you!

- Preserve the top tier of your wedding cake for your first anniversary.

- Send a special gift to both sets of parents, such as a small album containing the best photographs of the wedding. Personalize this gift by having it engraved.

DON'TS

- Don't get involved in other activities; you will be very busy planning your wedding.

- Don't make any major decisions without discussing them openly with your fiancé.

- Don't be controlling. Be open to other people's ideas.

- Don't overspend your budget!

- Don't try to impress your friends.

- Don't wait until the last minute to hire your service providers. The good ones get booked months in advance.

- Don't try to make everyone happy; it is impossible and will only make your wedding planning more difficult.

- Don't try to do everything. Delegate responsibilities to your fiancé, your parents, and to members of your wedding party.

- Don't rely on friends or family to photograph or record your wedding. Hire professionals!

- Don't assume that members of your wedding party know what to do. Give them direction with your Wedding Party Timeline and the *Wedding Party Responsibility Cards*, available at most major bookstores.

- Don't assume your service providers know what to do. Give each of them a copy of your detailed Service Provider Timeline.

- Don't schedule your bachelorette party the night before the wedding. You don't want to have a hangover on your special day!

DO'S & DON'TS

- Don't arrive late to the ceremony!

- Don't drink too much during the reception. Have a glass of water between each drink.

- Don't rub cake in the face of your spouse during the cake-cutting ceremony; your spouse might not appreciate it!

- Don't leave your reception without saying goodbye to your family and friends.

WEDDING PARTY RESPONSIBILITIES

Each member of your wedding party has his or her own individual duties and responsibilities. The following is a list of the most important duties for each member of your wedding party.

The most convenient method for conveying this information to members of your wedding party is by purchasing a set of the *Wedding Party Responsibility Cards*, published by WS Publishing Group.

These cards are attractive and contain all the information your wedding party needs to know to assure a smooth wedding: what to do, how to do it, when to do it, when to arrive, and much more. They also include financial responsibilities as well as the processional, recessional, and altar lineup. This book is available at most major bookstores.

MAID OF HONOR

- Helps bride select attire and address invitations.
- Plans bridal shower.
- Arrives at dressing site two hours before ceremony to assist bride in dressing.
- Arrives dressed at ceremony site one hour before the wedding for photographs.
- Arranges the bride's veil and train before the processional and recessional.
- Holds bride's bouquet and groom's ring, if no ring bearer, during the ceremony.
- Witnesses the signing of the marriage license.
- Keeps bride on schedule.
- Dances with best man during the bridal party dance.
- Helps bride change into her going away clothes.
- Mails wedding announcements after the wedding.
- Returns bridal slip, if rented.

BRIDESMAIDS

- Assists maid of honor in planning bridal shower.
- Assists bride with errands and addressing invitations.
- Participates in all pre-wedding parties.
- Arrives at dressing site two hours before ceremony.
- Arrives dressed at ceremony site one hour before the wedding for photographs.

- Walks behind ushers in order of height during the processional, either in pairs or in single file.
- Sits next to ushers at the head table.
- Dances with ushers and other important guests.
- Encourages single women to participate in the bouquet-tossing ceremony.

BRIDE'S MOTHER

- Helps prepare guest list for bride and her family.
- Helps plan the wedding ceremony and reception.
- Helps bride select her bridal gown.
- Helps bride keep track of gifts received.
- Selects her own attire according to the formality and color of the wedding.
- Makes accommodations for bride's out-of-town guests.
- Arrives dressed at ceremony site one hour before the wedding for photographs.
- Is the last person to be seated right before the processional begins.
- Sits in the left front pew to the left of bride's father during the ceremony.
- May stand up to signal the start of the processional.
- Can witness the signing of the marriage license.
- Dances with the groom after the first dance.
- Acts as hostess at the reception.

BRIDE'S FATHER

- Helps prepare guest list for bride and her family.
- Selects attire that complements groom's attire.
- Rides to the ceremony with bride in limousine.
- Arrives dressed at ceremony site one hour before the wedding for photographs.
- After giving bride away, sits in the left front pew to the right of bride's mother. If divorced, sits in second or third row unless financing the wedding.
- When officiant asks, "Who gives this bride away?" answers, "Her mother and I do," or something similar.
- Can witness the signing of the marriage license.
- Dances with bride after first dance.
- Acts as host at the reception.

FLOWER GIRL

- Attends rehearsal to practice, but is not required to attend pre-wedding parties.
- Arrives dressed at ceremony site 45 minutes before the wedding for photos.
- Carries a basket filled with loose rose petals to strew along bride's path during processional, if allowed by ceremony site.
- If very young, may sit with her parents during ceremony.

RING BEARER

- Attends rehearsal to practice but is not required to attend pre-wedding parties.
- Arrives at ceremony site 45 minutes before the wedding for photographs.
- Carries a white pillow with rings attached.
- If younger than seven years, carries mock rings.
- If very young, may sit with his parents during ceremony.
- If mock rings are used, turns the ring pillow over at the end of the ceremony.

NOTES

TIMELINES

The following section includes two different timelines or schedule of events for your wedding day: one for members of your wedding party and one for the various service providers you have hired. Use these timelines to help your wedding party and service providers understand their roles and where they need to be throughout your wedding day. This will also give you a much better idea of how your special day will unfold.

When preparing your timeline, first list the time that your wedding ceremony will begin. Then work forward or backwards, using the sample as your guide. The samples included give you an idea of how much time each event typically takes. But feel free to change the amount of time allotted for any event when customizing your own.

SAMPLE WEDDING PARTY TIMELINE

This is a sample wedding party timeline. To develop your own, use the blank form in this chapter, then make copies and give one to each member of your wedding party.

TIME	DESCRIPTION	BRIDE	BRIDE'S MOTHER	BRIDE'S FATHER	MAID OF HONOR	BRIDESMAIDS	BRIDE'S FAMILY	GROOM	GROOM'S MOTHER	GROOM'S FATHER	BEST MAN	USHERS	GROOM'S FAMILY	FLOWER GIRL	RING BEARER
2:30 PM	Hair/makeup appointment	✓	✓		✓	✓									
4:30 PM	Arrive at dressing site							✓			✓	✓			
5:15 PM	Arrive at ceremony site							✓	✓	✓	✓	✓	✓		
5:15 PM	Pre-ceremony photos	✓	✓	✓	✓	✓	✓								
5:30 PM	Ushers distribute wedding programs											✓			
5:30 PM	Prelude music begins														
5:45 PM	Ushers seat honored guests											✓			
5:50 PM	Ushers seat groom's parents								✓	✓		✓			
5:55 PM	Ushers seat bride's mother		✓									✓			
5:55 PM	Attendants line up for procession			✓	✓							✓		✓	✓
5:56 PM	Bride's father takes his place next to bride	✓		✓											
5:58 PM	Groom's party enters							✓			✓				
6:00 PM	Processional music begins														

TIME	DESCRIPTION	BRIDE	BRIDE'S MOTHER	BRIDE'S FATHER	MAID OF HONOR	BRIDESMAIDS	BRIDE'S FAMILY	GROOM	GROOM'S MOTHER	GROOM'S FATHER	BEST MAN	USHERS	GROOM'S FAMILY	FLOWER GIRL	RING BEARER
6:20 PM	Wedding party marches down aisle	✓			✓			✓			✓			✓	✓
6:25 PM	Sign marriage certificate	✓			✓			✓			✓				
6:30 PM	Post-ceremony photos taken	✓	✓	✓	✓	✓	✓	✓	✓	✓	✓	✓	✓	✓	✓
6:30 PM	Cocktails and hors d'oeuvres served														
7:45 PM	Guests are seated and dinner is served														
8:30 PM	Toasts are given										✓				
8:40 PM	First dance	✓						✓							
9:40 PM	Cake-cutting ceremony	✓						✓							
10:00 PM	Bride tosses bouquet to single women	✓			✓	✓								✓	
10:10 PM	Groom removes garter from bride's leg	✓						✓							
10:15 PM	Groom tosses garter to single men							✓			✓	✓			✓
10:45 PM	Bride and groom make grand exit	✓						✓							

WEDDING PARTY TIMELINE

Create your own timeline using this form. Make copies and give one to each member of your wedding party.

TIME	DESCRIPTION	BRIDE	BRIDE'S MOTHER	BRIDE'S FATHER	MAID OF HONOR	BRIDESMAIDS	BRIDE'S FAMILY	GROOM	GROOM'S MOTHER	GROOM'S FATHER	BEST MAN	USHERS	GROOM'S FAMILY	FLOWER GIRL	RING BEARER

TIME	DESCRIPTION	BRIDE	BRIDE'S MOTHER	BRIDE'S FATHER	MAID OF HONOR	BRIDESMAIDS	BRIDE'S FAMILY	GROOM	GROOM'S MOTHER	GROOM'S FATHER	BEST MAN	USHERS	GROOM'S FAMILY	FLOWER GIRL	RING BEARER

This is a sample of a service provider timeline. To develop your own, use the blank form in this chapter, then make copies and give one to each one of your service providers.

TIME	DESCRIPTION	BAKER	CATERER	CEREMONY MUSICIANS	OTHER	FLORIST	HAIRSTYLIST	MAKEUP ARTIST	PARTY RENTALS	PHOTOGRAPHER	RECEPTION MUSICIANS	VIDEOGRAPHER
1:00 PM	Supplies delivered to ceremony site								✓			
1:30 PM	Supplies delivered to reception site								✓			
2:30 PM	Makeup artist meets bride at:							✓				
3:00 PM	Hairstylist meets bride at:						✓					
4:15 PM	Caterer begins setting up		✓									
4:40 PM	Baker delivers cake to reception site	✓										
4:45 PM	Pre-ceremony photos of groom's family at:									✓		
5:00 PM	Videographer arrives at ceremony site											✓
5:15 PM	Pre-ceremony photos of bride's family at:									✓		
5:20 PM	Ceremony site decorations finalized				✓	✓						
5:30 PM	Prelude music begins			✓								
5:45 PM	Reception site decorations finalized		✓		✓	✓						
6:30 PM	Post-ceremony photos at:									✓		
6:30 PM	Band or DJ begins playing										✓	

TIME	DESCRIPTION	BAKER	CATERER	CEREMONY MUSICIANS	OTHER	FLORIST	HAIRSTYLIST	LIMOUSINE	PARTY RENTALS	PHOTOGRAPHER	RECEPTION MUSICIANS	VIDEOGRAPHER
6:30 PM	Transport guest book/gifts to reception site				✓							
6:45 PM	Move arch/urns/flowers to reception site				✓							
7:00 PM	Limo picks up bride/groom at ceremony site							✓				
7:15 PM	DJ announces entrance of bride and groom										✓	
7:45 PM	Dinner is served		✓									
8:15 PM	Champagne served for toasts		✓									
8:30 PM	Band/DJ announces toast by best man										✓	
8:40 PM	Band/DJ announces first dance										✓	
9:00 PM	Transport gifts to:				✓							
9:30 PM	Band/DJ announces cake-cutting ceremony										✓	
10:30 PM	Transport top tier of cake, cake-top, etc. to:				✓							
10:40 PM	Transport rental items to:				✓							
10:45 PM	Limo picks up bride/groom at reception site							✓				
11:45 PM	Picks up supplies at ceremony/reception sites								✓			

SERVICE PROVIDER TIMELINE

Create your own timeline using this form. Make copies and give one to each of your service providers.

TIME	DESCRIPTION	BAKER	CATERER	CEREMONY MUSICIANS	OFFICIANT	OTHER	FLORIST	HAIRSTYLIST	LIMOUSINE	MAKEUP ARTIST	MANICURIST	PARTY RENTALS	PHOTOGRAPHER	RECEPTION MUSICIANS	VIDEOGRAPHER

TIME	DESCRIPTION	BAKER	CATERER	CEREMONY MUSICIANS	OFFICIANT	OTHER	FLORIST	HAIRSTYLIST	LIMOUSINE	MAKEUP ARTIST	MANICURIST	PARTY RENTALS	PHOTOGRAPHER	RECEPTION MUSICIANS	VIDEOGRAPHER

NOTES

_____

_____

_____

_____

_____

_____

_____

_____

_____

_____

_____

_____

_____

_____

_____

_____

_____

_____

_____

_____

_____

_____

_____

_____

_____

_____

_____

_____

WHO PAYS FOR WHAT

BRIDE AND/OR BRIDE'S FAMILY

- Engagement party
- Wedding consultant's fee
- Bridal gown, veil, and accessories
- Wedding stationery, calligraphy, and postage
- Wedding gift for bridal couple
- Groom's wedding ring
- Gifts for bridesmaids
- Bridesmaids' bouquets
- Pre-wedding parties and bridesmaids' luncheon
- Photography and videography
- Bride's medical exam and blood test
- Wedding guest book and other accessories
- Total cost of the ceremony, including location, flowers, music, rental items, and accessories
- Total cost of the reception, including location, flowers, music, rental items, accessories, food, beverages, cake, decorations, favors, etc.

- Transportation for bridal party to ceremony and reception
- Own attire and travel expenses

ATTENDANTS

- Own attire except flowers
- Travel expenses
- Bridal shower
- Bachelorette party
- Gift for bride and groom

WEDDING FORMATIONS

The following section illustrates the typical ceremony formations (Processional, Recessional and Altar Line Up) for both Christian and Jewish weddings, as well as the typical formations for the Receiving Line, Head Table and Parents' Tables at the reception.

✠LTAR ℒINE 𝒰P

ABBREVIATIONS

B=Bride	GF=Groom's Father	G=Groom
BM=Best Man	BMa=Bridesmaids	MH=Maid of Honor
BF=Bride's Father	OR=Other Relatives	BMo=Bride's Mother
O=Officiant	U=Ushers	GM=Groom's Mother

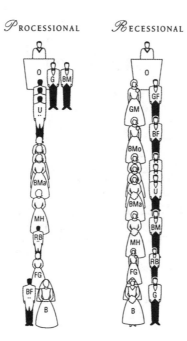

*P*ROCESSIONAL   *R*ECESSIONAL

ABBREVIATIONS

B=Bride	GF=Groom's Father	G=Groom
BM=Best Man	BMa=Bridesmaids	MH=Maid of Honor
BF=Bride's Father	OR=Other Relatives	BMo=Bride's Mother
O=Officiant	U=Ushers	GM=Groom's Mother

Altar Line Up

ABBREVIATIONS

B=Bride
BM=Best Man
BF=Bride's Father
O=Officiant

GF=Groom's Father
BMa=Bridesmaids
OR=Other Relatives
U=Ushers

G=Groom
MH=Maid of Honor
BMo=Bride's Mother
GM=Groom's Mother

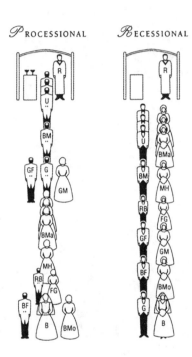

*P*ROCESSIONAL   *R*ECESSIONAL

ABBREVIATIONS

B=Bride   GF=Groom's Father   G=Groom
BM=Best Man   BMa=Bridesmaids   MH=Maid of Honor
BF=Bride's Father   OR=Other Relatives   BMo=Bride's Mother
O=Officiant   U=Ushers   GM=Groom's Mother

WEDDING FORMATIONS

RECEIVING LINE

BMo BF GM GF B G MH BMa BMa BMa

HEAD TABLE

BMa U BMa BM. B G MH U BMa U

PARENTS' TABLE

ABBREVIATIONS

B=Bride	GF=Groom's Father	G=Groom
BM=Best Man	BMa=Bridesmaids	MH=Maid of Honor
BF=Bride's Father	OR=Other Relatives	BMo=Bride's Mother
O=Officiant	U=Ushers	GM=Groom's Mother

WeddingSolutions.com

Everything You Need to Plan Your Dream Wedding

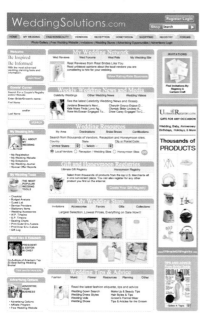

- The Latest Wedding Gowns
- Comprehensive Wedding Planning Tools
- Articles, Tips & Advice
- Thousands of Local Vendors
- Beautiful Reception Sites
- Honeymoon Destinations
- Largest Online Wedding Store
- Wedding Forums
- Personal Wedding Website
- Honeymoon & Gift Registry
- Polls, News, Videos, Media
- Wedding Planning Certification Programs

SEARCH FOR WEDDING GOWNS
View the Latest Designs

Search for your perfect wedding gown by designer, style and price.

SEARCH FOR RESOURCES
Reputable & Reliable

Find local vendors, reception, honeymoon & destination wedding sites.

Log on to www.WeddingSolutions.com for more information

WeddingSolutions.com

$99 Value

FREE Wedding Website
on WeddingSolutions.com

Includes 19 Custom Pages

- Wedding Party
- Registry
- Local Info
- City Guide
- Home
- Our Story
- Photo Gallery
- Details of Events
- Accommodations
- Things to Do
- Restaurants
- Guest Book
- View Guest Book
- Sign Guest Book
- Wedding Journal
- Honeymoon
- Miscellaneous
- RSVP
- Contact Us

SAVE UP TO $200 ON WEDDING INVITATIONS & ACCESSORIES

Invitations............................

SAVE up to $100

- Wedding Invitations
- Engagement
- Bridal Shower
- Rehearsal Dinner
- Casual Wedding
- Seal 'n Send
- Save The Date
- Maps/Direction Cards
- Programs
- Thank-You Notes
- Much More!

Accessories............................

SAVE up to $100

- Toasting Glasses
- Attendants' Gifts
- Unity Candles
- Aisle Runners
- Cake Tops
- Flower Girl Basket
- Ring Pillow
- Guest Book
- Cake Knife & Server
- Favors
- Much More!

Log on to www.WeddingSolutions.com/specialoffers
for more details on these offers

WedSpace.com

THE BEST WAY TO PLAN YOUR ENTIRE WEDDING!

‹ **Wedding Journal**
Share your Love Story: All about you and your partner, how you met and got engaged. Upload photos and videos, inform your guests on pre-wedding parties, where to stay, local info, and more.

‹ **Photo Slideshow**
Share your photos with friends and family!

‹ **Create a Network**
Engaged couples, wedding guests, wedding vendors, family and friends.

‹ **Wedding Wall**
Share, connect and discover! Exchange ideas and view photos and videos. Chat with vendors, get advice from real brides and much more.

Guests Can Meet
Your wedding guests can chat and share media before, during, and after the wedding.

I'm the bride's cousin!

What hotel are you staying at?

Let's meet after the wedding.

Facebook Connect
You can easily transfer your Facebook friends, wall, and photos to WedSpace and invite your friends to view your journal.

Log on to WedSpace.com to create your FREE Wedding Journal today!

WedSpace.com

FREE Online Wedding Journal!
$29.95 Value

A fun and exciting way to share your Love Story and Wedding Details with friends and family.

Celebrating the Wedding of
Chelsea & Trever

June 10th, 2011 • 348 days to go!

Friend Request Send to Friend Send Message Send E-Card Invite to Group Add to Favorites

HOME   OUR STORY   WEDDING DETAILS   REGISTRY   RSVP   MEDIA   VIEW OUR

Welcome to our Wedding Journal!

To read our love story, view our wedding details, see where we have registered, RSVP and so much more, simply log in or register and click on "Friend Request." You will be able to read our Wedding Wall/blog, meet our wedding vendors and other guests who are coming to the wedding, and so much more.

Answer quick questions and upload photos and videos to customize pages including:

- All About Him
- All About Her
- How We Met

- Our Engagement
- Ceremony Details
- Reception Details

- Where to Stay
- And much more

The perfect tool for your guests to RSVP for your wedding and find out where you have registered!

Create Your FREE Online Wedding Journal Today!
(Use discount code "FREE3369" during registration)